-*Living*-
Beyond Your Capacity

UNDERSTANDING THE

SPIRIT-FILLED LIFE

Paul Chappell

First published in 2010 by Striving Together Publications, a
ministry of Lancaster Baptist Church, Lancaster, CA 93535.
Striving Together Publications is committed to providing
tried, trusted, and proven books that will further equip local
churches to carry out the Great Commission. Your comments
and suggestions are valued.

Striving Together Publications
4020 E. Lancaster Blvd.
Lancaster, CA 93535
800.201.7748

Cover design by Andrew Jones
Layout by Craig Parker
Edited by Cary Schmidt, Amanda Michael, Monica Bass
Special thanks to our proofreaders

ISBN 978-1-59894-108-1

Printed in the United States of America

This book is dedicated to Dr. and Mrs. Don Sisk.
Thank you for living and ministering by His Spirit
throughout your life and ministry.

CONTENTS

ACKNOWLEDGMENTS

I would like to first acknowledge Dr. Lee Roberson for his personal challenges to me regarding the importance of the Spirit-filled life.

I would like to thank Brother Cary Schmidt for
taking this project from start to finish and making it a reality.
I appreciate his desire to apply these truths personally and then to
share them in our needy generation.

I also wish to thank Monica Bass and Amanda Michael for their
research and editorial assistance for this book.

FOREWORD

Twenty-six years ago, the Lord providentially intersected my life with Paul Chappell. Little did I know what God had in store for my future through the ministry of this man. Words fail to express the spiritual impact of his life upon me and my family.

For twenty of those years, God has privileged me to serve on the staff of Lancaster Baptist Church under Pastor Chappell's leadership. For all of these years, I've had the opportunity to see him in thousands of circumstances—the good days, the hard days, the blessed days, the sorrowful days, the stressful days, and everything in between. We've laughed together frequently, rejoiced together abundantly, and wept together occasionally. I've seen him attacked and applauded. I've watched him face every kind of circumstance of life.

Through it all, I've seen a Spirit-filled life.

In my thirty-five-years as a Christian, I've never met a better living testament of the power and presence of the Holy Spirit in the life of a man. In that, I do not imply that I have seen perfection. But I have seen the continual, relentless pursuit of a spiritual life in every possible application. I have watched a man unrelentingly surrender and submit to the Spirit's guidance. I have seen sincerity, passion, holiness, authenticity, consistency, and grace personified in his personal life, his family life, his public life, his ministry leadership, and his unabated heart for souls. Frankly, his life and his walk are convicting and challenging.

The results speak for themselves. God is using Pastor Paul Chappell in a remarkable way. I am grateful to witness the evident outpouring of God's blessing on his life. But I am eternally more grateful for what I have witnessed "off the platform" in his genuine, Spirit-filled heart.

One reason I believe this book will bless you greatly is that it flows from a life that is living its message every day. Thank you, Pastor, for living "beyond your capacity" and showing us all that God still does the impossible through surrendered vessels.

Cary Schmidt

June 2010

TRANSCENDENT COMPANIONSHIP

Have you ever taken a long walk with a very good friend? Have you cherished the presence of someone you love, perhaps while sitting beside a crackling fire, sipping a cup of hot tea? If so, you understand the closeness, the encouragement, and the depth of a relationship that can unfold at such times. Moments such as these strengthen you. They breathe life into your soul. They lift you—emotionally and spiritually—to a place where you could not take yourself.

The book you hold is designed to create such moments between you and a very dear Friend, to whom I would like to introduce to you. Whether you meet Him for the first time in these pages, or whether you have walked with Him for many years, I pray that you will draw closer to Him because of our time together. He loves you. He longs to become your dearest companion and guide, and His powerful presence will change everything in your life for the better.

Every human being is born with the inherent longing for companionship, and every heart craves a companionship that no human being can provide. While we cherish the closeness of family and friends, these earthly relationships ultimately fall short, for no single person can fill the heart with joy, stability, strength, and purpose. No flesh and blood can provide eternal resources to the soul and spirit.

The deepest of desires in each of us calls for a *transcendent companion*—one who defies the boundaries of time, space, and finiteness. He is one who knows you intimately and loves you unconditionally. He is the only one who could care for you eternally, sustain you limitlessly, strengthen you abundantly, and lead you perfectly through this life.

He is the Holy Spirit of God. He is real. He is the third person of the Godhead. He is God's gracious gift to you every moment of every day. And He is waiting to lead you into a life of abundance— abundant joy, abundant peace, abundant purpose, abundant strength, and abundant grace. He is God's eternal presence *in* your life and God's eternal resource *for* your life. He is the ultimate fulfillment of your deepest desire for *transcendent companionship*!

Once He comes into your life, He will never leave you and never forsake you.

For nearly forty years, He has been my companion. Learning to walk with Him is an ongoing process. I'm sure I could live ten lifetimes and still have much to learn about hearing His voice, obeying His prompting, and trusting His leadership. I do not pretend to write this book from a full understanding or a flawless perspective of "Spirit-filled living." Rather, I write from within the daily struggle—from the minutia of moment-by-moment efforts to submit to His presence and rely upon His power.

My walk with Him has not been without failure, but it *has* been genuine. This wonderful companion is truly my dearest friend. He is the first one I speak to each morning and the last one I speak to each night. Our conversation lasts all day, and truly without Him, I would not want to face a single day. Life apart from Him is frustrating, overwhelming, and purposeless. The best days of my Christian life have been the days when He was in complete control. And the worst days have been the ones in which He was grieved or quenched. Without a doubt, whatever good has come about in my life, family, or ministry is *His* doing, not my own.

When God created Adam, He breathed life into him. He was spiritually alive and in close communion with God. But not many days later, Adam and Eve chose to sin. In spite of God's warning, "thou shalt surely die…" (Genesis 2:17), they chose spiritual death. From that time forward, the human race has been born into spiritual separation from God (Romans 5:12). In other words, God's Spirit no longer automatically resides within us because of our sinful nature. By nature, we are walking dead people, spiritually speaking.

In essence, you were created to live every day with the abiding presence of God's Holy Spirit inside of you. But because of sin, that relationship was cut off, and mankind was separated from fellowship and closeness with God.

Thanks to the Cross of Jesus Christ, the perfect Son of God, our sin was paid in full by His blood, and we have been invited back into a close relationship with God—for now and for eternity. By faith and trust, we can accept Jesus Christ as Saviour, and God's Holy Spirit can enter our lives. We can once again know God on a personal and intimate level.

Most Christians never really embrace this relationship. Even after the moment of salvation, many Christians continue living below their capacity. They fail to understand and authentically live in light of the transcendent companionship of the Holy Spirit. They walk through life, day after day, ignoring all that He is and desires to be, and relying instead on their own plans and their own strength. It is the ultimate picture of pathetic living—finite humans indwelled by infinite God, crawling and clawing through life in their own frailty, rather than soaring on the wings of divine enabling.

Are you tired of depending upon yourself? Are you looking for God? If you've found Him, are you eager to know Him more intimately? Wouldn't you like to experience Him personally and know that His almighty power is intervening in your life today?

Would you like to live beyond your capacity?

The wonderful Holy Spirit of God desires to come into your life at salvation, and unfold a daily work of power, grace, and transformation. In every way, He desires to enable you to live a supernatural life—a life that exceeds your humanity and expresses His Divinity.

In Isaiah 40:28–31, God gives these words, "Hast thou not known? hast thou not heard, that the everlasting God, the LORD, the Creator of the ends of the earth, fainteth not, neither is weary? there is no searching of his understanding. He giveth power to the faint; and to them that have no might he increaseth strength. Even the youths shall faint and be weary, and the young men shall utterly fall: But they that wait upon the LORD shall renew their strength; they shall mount up with wings as eagles; they shall run, and not be weary; and they shall walk, and not faint."

This is living beyond your capacity. This is the result of coming to the end of yourself and depending utterly upon the Spirit of God. Life with the Holy Spirit is not a fainting, faltering, weary life. It is a strength increasing, mounting up, soaring life. And while I have yet to perfectly attain, I earnestly desire to live this life today. I believe you do too.

And so, with this yearning for transcendent companionship, I invite you to meet and develop a relationship with the Holy Spirit of God.

A.W. Tozer spoke of Him this way, "The Holy Spirit is a person. He is not enthusiasm. He is not courage. He is not energy. He is not the personification of all good qualities, like Jack Frost is the personification of cold weather. Actually, the Holy Spirit is not the personification of anything—He has individuality. He is one being and not another. He has will and intelligence. He has hearing. He has knowledge and sympathy and ability to love and see and think. He can hear, speak, desire, grieve and rejoice. He is a Person."

He is my companion. And He desires to be yours as well. For many, He is an oft-neglected friend. My prayer is that this book will forever improve your relationship with Him.

Take a walk with Him through these pages. Sit by the warmth of His presence, and get to know Him more deeply and dependently. I will do my best to portray Him in the light of Scripture—but try to ignore *me* and see *Him*! Then, begin to follow His leading, and trust His enabling every day. Truly, He alone can fill the longing of your heart and lift you to a life beyond your capacity.

PART ONE
THE MINISTRY OF THE HOLY SPIRIT

WHO IS THE HOLY SPIRIT?

WHAT IS HE LIKE?

HOW DOES HE THINK?

AND WHAT IS HIS PURPOSE?

To understand the mighty Spirit of God,
we will examine the incredible ways
that God describes Him in His Word…

ONE

HIS SAVING MINISTRY

The summer of 1983 marked the beginning of my full-time ministry. My wife Terrie and I had recently completed Bible college and joined the pastoral staff of a dynamic church. With a fresh haircut, a suit, a Bible, a college degree, and a cubicle, I was eager to serve God in local church ministry. One of my early experiences involved an Indian couple named Hemat and Nanda.

They had called the church asking for marriage counseling, and I was eager to reach couples. So, despite the fact that I had never conducted any marriage counseling, I offered to meet with them in my spacious cubicle at the church office.

I will never forget that appointment. As we sat down, it was clear that Hemat and Nanda had tremendous tension and anger toward each other.

"How long have you been married?" I asked innocently.

"Ten years," he answered coldly.

I continued, "And what seems to be the problem that you are facing right now?"

She sternly replied, "I hate him."

"And I hate her," he echoed.

"I see," I paused, a bit taken back, "And how long have you experienced these problems?"

"Ten years," they both stated.

Talk about baptism by fire! They hadn't taught me about this scenario in Bible college. As the story unfolded, I learned that Hemat and Nanda had an arranged marriage. Ten years prior, their fathers in India had met at a market, struck a deal, and bargained for their union. Not only had they never been in love, they never even *liked* each other.

With a bit of trepidation, I opened my Bible and began to share the Gospel of Jesus Christ with Hemat and Nanda. They had a Hindu background and were used to thinking in terms of thousands of gods. What a joy it was to explain the One true and living God, and His gracious desire to save them and come into their lives. I shared how this One God sent His only begotten Son to die on a cross. I showed them how His death on the Cross was the full payment for their sins. I explained that their sins separated them from God, and invited them to trust Jesus Christ alone to be their Saviour.

They listened hesitantly, but as I shared the Word of God, I could see a work unfolding in their lives that was beyond human ability. Their countenances softened. Their hearts changed. Right before my eyes, the Holy Spirit of God was beginning His first and most important ministry within this dear couple—the ministry of *salvation*.

His work took time, for Hemat and Nanda did not accept Christ that day. But the seed of God's Word found the fertile soil of their hearts, and several weeks later, after multiple appointments, they both bowed their heads, turned away from their false gods, and accepted Jesus Christ as their personal Saviour. It was one of the first of hundreds of times that I would witness the Holy Spirit performing the miracle of salvation.

As we begin to understand the Holy Spirit—our first stop on the journey is salvation. This chapter has two purposes:

First, if you have never come to a moment of salvation when you turned from sin and false gods to trust the only Saviour, Jesus Christ, I pray you will make this decision. To have the Holy Spirit in your life, you must first be "born again" by the Holy Spirit.

The term *born again* appears in Scripture when a very religious and curious man came to Jesus in John 3. Jesus said these words to him in verses 5–7, "Verily, verily, I say unto thee, Except a man be born of water and of the Spirit, he cannot enter into the kingdom of God. That which is born of the flesh is flesh; and that which is born of the Spirit is spirit. Marvel not that I said unto thee, Ye must be born again."

To be *born again* is to be made spiritually alive by God's Spirit—to be saved. Are you saved? If not, I pray you will listen to God's Holy Spirit as you read on. More importantly, I pray you will accept His invitation to be "born of the Spirit."

Second, if you are already saved, the purpose of this chapter is to remind you that the first passion and ministry of the Holy Spirit in your life is to fully express your salvation that you might help others understand the Gospel and come to Christ.

It is awesome to think that God would take a personal interest in every single living soul, inviting them into an eternal, intimate relationship with Him. He has created each of us with a free will to choose or reject Him, but that does not stop Him from extending the invitation and drawing us to Christ. Let's discover the ministry of the Holy Spirit in saving the human soul.

THE HOLY SPIRIT INVITES

Revelation 22:17 states, "And the Spirit and the bride say, Come. And let him that heareth say, Come. And let him that is athirst come. And whosoever will, let him take the water of life freely."

Religions all over the world hold people hostage to performance-based acceptance. Millions of people really believe that the only way to be accepted of God is to atone for their own sins by doing good works or religious deeds. But this is not the work of the Spirit of God. Simply put, God's Spirit says, "Come! Whosoever will… take of the water of life *freely*." Again God says in Romans 6:23, "…the *gift* of God is eternal life." Throughout the Bible, God's Spirit invites thirsty souls to place their faith in Jesus Christ. He does not require baptism, church membership, financial donations, or a list of good deeds. He does not demand adherence to a religious system nor does He force us to atone for sins or earn salvation. He *invites*—one and all, young and old, rich and poor, good and bad. Everyone needs a Saviour, and anyone who will may come.

A pastor in California was giving an invitation at the end of his Sunday morning message when a five-year-old boy, sensing the invitation of the Holy Spirit, came down the aisle.

Not knowing if the boy was old enough to understand salvation, the pastor took him to his office and began to ask some theological questions. The more he questioned, the more confused the boy became. Finally, in exasperation, the little fellow stopped and innocently pleaded, "Pastor Patterson, in your message this morning you said that if I would come and ask Jesus to save me— He would! Now, did you really mean that or not?!" The pastor said, "I didn't ask him any more questions after that." He helped the boy respond to God's invitation by inviting Jesus Christ to be his Saviour.

Frankly, the complexity of man-made religions overshadows the simplicity of God's invitation.

THE HOLY SPIRIT CONVICTS

Jesus said of the Holy Spirit in John 16:8, "And when he is come, he will reprove the world of sin, and of righteousness, and of judgment."

Have you ever wondered what makes mankind aware of right and wrong? Have you ever considered that people all over the world inherently worship something or someone? The basic knowledge of God and the knowledge of right and wrong are woven into the fiber of our conscience. Creator God has placed these things within us that we might respond to Him. And then, by His Spirit, He works through our conscience to convict or convince us of our need for Him.

> The complexity of man-made religions overshadows the simplicity of God's invitation.

He reproves or convicts us of three basic things—sin, righteousness, and judgment. He reminds us that we are sinful beings by nature, and He convicts us of the sin of rejecting Christ. He teaches us of the *righteousness* of Jesus Christ, the Son of God, and that we fall short of God's perfect righteous standard.

And He convicts us of the *judgment* that is reserved for unbelievers, and calls us to avoid God's judgment by trusting Christ and His payment for our sins.

In Acts 9:5, the Holy Spirit was performing this convicting work in the heart of an angry, Christian-hating man named Saul. He ultimately said to Saul, "…it is hard for thee to kick against the pricks." Saul was a man trying to fight off the conviction of the Holy Spirit in his heart.

Are you doing that right now? Do you sense the Spirit of God inviting you into a relationship with Him? Do you sense a growing awareness of your sin, your need for Christ's righteousness, and a desire to avoid God's judgment? That is God's Spirit bringing conviction into your heart. It is His very touch—His voice—leading you to a change of mind about yourself as a sinner and Jesus as the Saviour. Whatever you do, don't "kick against the pricks." Answer His invitation with a resounding, "YES!"

THE HOLY SPIRIT REGENERATES

Titus 3:5 says, "Not by works of righteousness which we have done, but according to his mercy he saved us, by the washing of regeneration, and renewing of the Holy Ghost."

Not only does the Spirit of God invite you to be saved and convict you of your need for a Saviour, but at the moment you accept Christ, He *regenerates* you. He brings you to life spiritually. The word *regenerate* means to re-gene. It means that God gives you a complete and total spiritual renovation.

Another word the Bible uses for this is *quicken*, which means to make alive. Romans 8:11 says, "But if the Spirit of him that raised up Jesus from the dead dwell in you, he that raised up Christ from the dead shall also quicken your mortal bodies by his Spirit that dwelleth in you."

What an amazing thought! God offers new life to anyone who will simply accept it by faith. His Holy Spirit offers to bring to life (in you) what died so long ago when Adam and Eve sinned in the Garden of Eden. This regeneration is the beginning point of a relationship with God—being spiritually reborn into His family and becoming His child.

Written to a group of people who had recently made the decision to trust Christ as Saviour, 1 Corinthians 6:10–11 describes it this way, "Nor thieves, nor covetous, nor drunkards, nor revilers, nor extortioners, shall inherit the kingdom of God. And such were some of you: but ye are washed, but ye are sanctified, but ye are justified in the name of the Lord Jesus, and by the Spirit of our God."

The story is told of a young lady who accepted Christ as her Saviour and applied for membership in a local Bible-believing church. "Were you a sinner before you received the Lord Jesus into your life?" inquired an old deacon.

"Yes, sir," she replied.

"Well, are you still a sinner?"

"To tell you the truth, I feel I'm a greater sinner than ever."

"Then what real change have you experienced?"

"I don't quite know how to explain it," she said, "except that I used to be a sinner running *after* sin, but now that I am saved, I'm a sinner running *from* sin!"

God desires to give every person a new birth, a new life, a new heart, and a new purpose. It all happens when His Holy Spirit is allowed to perform the marvelous miracle of *regeneration*. It happens in the simple moment of decision. You could make that decision right now, for the Bible says, "…whosoever shall call upon the name of the Lord shall be saved" (Romans 10:13).

THE HOLY SPIRIT INDWELLS

The miracle continues! Just when you think it couldn't possibly be any better, God places His Spirit inside of you. John 14:17 says, "Even the Spirit of truth; whom the world cannot receive, because it seeth him not, neither knoweth him: but ye know him; for he dwelleth with you, and shall be in you." Look at 1 Corinthians 3:16, "Know ye not that ye are the temple of God, and that the Spirit of God dwelleth in you?" And 2 Corinthians 1:22 promises the Holy

Spirit will dwell in our hearts, "Who hath also sealed us, and given the earnest of the Spirit in our hearts."

These verses and many more teach us an incredible reality— God is in us. This is where *living beyond your capacity* really begins. At the moment you invite Christ into your heart, the very presence of God's Spirit takes up permanent residence in your life. From that moment on, you are the temple or dwelling place of His Spirit (1 Corinthians 6:19).

God says it again in Romans 8:9, "But ye are not in the flesh, but in the Spirit, if so be that the Spirit of God dwell in you. Now if any man have not the Spirit of Christ, he is none of his." Hence, you do not receive Christ at one point and then receive the Holy Spirit as a later event in your life. The Holy Spirit is with you beginning at salvation. This changes everything! We will spend the rest of this book examining exactly what it means to be "in the Spirit."

THE HOLY SPIRIT SEALS

How long am I saved? Can I lose my salvation? Can I ever be unsaved after I am saved? These are great questions, and many people struggle with the answers. Remember, your relationship with God is not performance based; it is faith based. His invitation is to *come*, not to *earn*.

With that in mind, God's Spirit comes to the rescue once again with the word *seal*. Look at Ephesians 1:13, "In whom ye also trusted, after that ye heard the word of truth, the gospel of your salvation: in whom also after that ye believed, ye were sealed with that holy Spirit of promise." At salvation, you are *sealed*. What exactly does this mean?

In ancient times, a seal was the stamp made by a signet or private mark from a ruling king to indicate security, preservation, and ownership. For instance, if a letter was sealed with the king's seal, it was proven to belong to him. The seal was an official stamp of ownership and authority.

In the same way, the Holy Spirit of God indwelling you at salvation becomes your seal. He is the stamp of God's ownership in your life. He is the evidence that you belong to Christ. And He is *permanent* proof that you are one of God's own children. When God seals you, that seal can never be undone by any power in Heaven or in Earth (Romans 8:31–39).

Another word that God uses to define this is *earnest*. Second Corinthians 1:22 reads, "Who hath also sealed us, and given the earnest of the Spirit in our hearts." This word means "down-payment." God's Holy Spirit in you is proof that He has purchased you by the blood of Christ and that you will one day spend all of eternity with Him.

THE HOLY SPIRIT RENEWS

Are you as amazed as I am at this point? What an awesome friend this Holy Spirit is already! But honestly, salvation is just the beginning. It's the start of a life-changing relationship. The Holy Spirit *in you* puts the power and wisdom of God at work in your heart on a daily basis. He brings all the strength and enabling of God to transform you from within—from who you *are* into who you *can be* with His help. This isn't about turning over a new leaf or getting a fresh start. It's not about surface or temporary change. It's about starting a complete spiritual renovation that will make you the person only God can help you to be.

Titus 3:5 speaks of this renewing work, "Not by works of righteousness which we have done, but according to his mercy he saved us, by the washing of regeneration, and renewing of the Holy Ghost." Second Corinthians 4:16 also mentions it, "For which cause we faint not; but though our outward man perish, yet the inward man is renewed day by day."

> The Holy Spirit *in you* puts the power and wisdom of God at work in your heart on a daily basis.

We will discover more about this renewing work later. Suffice to say, if you are tired of New Year's resolutions that never stick, bad habits that won't let go, and personal failures you can't seem to overcome,

God's Holy Spirit makes real and lasting life change both possible and probable.

THE HOLY SPIRIT GIVES ASSURANCE

The final aspect of the Holy Spirit's saving ministry is found in Romans 8:15–16, "For ye have not received the spirit of bondage again to fear; but ye have received the Spirit of adoption, whereby we cry, Abba, Father. The Spirit itself beareth witness with our spirit, that we are the children of God." The Holy Spirit of God gives us the assurance—the heart knowledge and affirmation—of salvation. He provides us with security—a security that is eternal and unchanging.

I recently came across this humorous story sent to Ann Landers regarding what it means to be adopted: "It happened again today. My two sons and I were in a shopping mall, and a total stranger felt the need to comment on the fact that my two boys didn't look anything alike. Apparently, my six year old decided it was time he explained the difference. 'I'm adopted,' he said. 'That's when you have the same family but not the same face.'"

Much like this little boy, if you have been saved, you were instantly adopted into God's family, and the Holy Spirit desires for you to live with absolute *certainty* of your security in God's love. He bears witness in your spirit that you belong to God and that

God accepts you—even *likes* you. You are His child and He is your Heavenly Father.

So many people live with the knowledge of God as a distant Deity, Sovereign over the universe—the all-powerful, all-knowing, eternal judge. But few know Him personally as a loving Heavenly Father and an intimate, faithful friend. This is how He longs for you to know Him. And it's all possible by His Spirit.

There's nothing on Earth like knowing the Lord Jesus Christ as your personal Saviour and having His Holy Spirit indwell your heart at salvation. The fact that God would come to live within me is an overwhelming and humbling thought. The Apostle Paul wrote of this in 2 Corinthians 4:7, "But we have this treasure in earthen vessels, that the excellency of the power may be of God, and not of us." God's Holy Spirit in your life brings infinite potential into your everyday limitations. He brings God's unlimited resources into your limited humanity. The implications are mind boggling! We've barely scratched the surface in this chapter. The coming pages are rich with the discovery of the multiplied blessings of God's Spirit in us.

God's Spirit *invites* you to Him, *convicts* you of your need, *regenerates* you through salvation, *indwells* your heart forever, *seals* you into God's family, *renews* your life day by day, and constantly *assures* you of God's love and acceptance. Do you see why I called Him a *transcendent companion*? No earthly relationship can fulfill these needs in your heart. Salvation really is an unspeakable gift from God (2 Corinthians 9:15).

AMAZING GRACE

In the early 1700s, John Newton was a cold-hearted, slave-trading man who had lived a life of hardness and sin. Those who knew him simultaneously feared him and hated him. He was a foul-mouthed, gambling drunk who cared little for life and who had given up on God in his childhood.

One stormy night at sea, God's Holy Spirit began working in John Newton's heart. After near shipwreck and drowning, Newton began to respond to God's conviction. A short time later, He accepted Christ as Saviour.

Beginning at that moment, the Holy Spirit of God completely transformed John Newton from a cold and heartless brute into a tender-hearted, gracious man. The change was astounding and inarguable. Eventually, God led Newton to become a faithful pastor and preacher in Olney, England, where he also wrote many well-known hymns with his friend William Cowper.

You know John Newton by his most well-known hymn—"Amazing Grace." I recently had the privilege of visiting Newton's church and reading his grave marker in Olney, England. It reads: "John Newton, Clerk [pastor], once an infidel and libertine, a servant of slaves in Africa, was, by the rich mercy of our Lord and Saviour Jesus Christ, preserved, restored, pardoned, and appointed to preach the faith he had long labored to destroy."

The saving ministry of the Holy Spirit is hard to adequately describe, but even harder to deny, especially when so evident in the life of a man like John Newton. Sin destroys, but God's Holy Spirit is eager to save and renew.

If we stopped here, my heart would be overwhelmed already, but salvation is just the beginning of the wonders of the Holy Spirit. Take a moment to thank God for His Spirit's saving work. And then let's continue our journey.

TWO

HIS SANCTIFYING MINISTRY

O n a cold and wintery December 16, 1944, nearly 600,000 American soldiers began a five-week fight that would be the single largest and bloodiest battle of World War II. Famously known as "The Battle of the Bulge," what began as a secret, massive German offensive near the small country of Luxembourg, ended in victory for the Allied forces. In the fighting, American troops suffered approximately 81,000 casualties, including 19,000 deaths.

Recently, I had the privilege of speaking for our missionaries in Germany. A friend took my wife and me to a fifty-acre plot of ground in Luxembourg known as the Luxembourg American Cemetery and Memorial. In this sacred place, we fought back tears and contemplated the great sacrifice made by American military men and women. My heart was overwhelmed by the more than five thousand white crosses that filled the landscape.

That fifty acres in Luxembourg is special. It's a place where people visit from all over the world to remember those who gave their lives for our freedom. It's a beautiful place, meticulously maintained, perfectly manicured, and distinctly serene and peaceful. In contrast to the battle it memorializes, it is strikingly calm and tranquil.

This is just one of twenty-four American cemeteries on foreign soil; and each one is hallowed ground where thousands of fallen soldiers are remembered. Each one is set apart—sanctified. Each plot of land represents the payment of American blood and stands set apart for the particular, sacred purpose of honoring that sacrifice.

In much the same fashion, when the miracle of salvation occurred, and the Holy Spirit indwelled your life, you were born into God's family and you became His precious, treasured child. By God's grace, He has set you apart—chosen you to live a life that pleases Him and honors the sacrifice of the blood of Christ on your behalf. And just as standing in that Luxembourg cemetery stirred within me a great desire to live an honorable life as an American, even so the sacrifice of Jesus Christ should compel us to live our lives in honor of Him. In a very practical sense, the Holy Spirit desires to make the inner work of salvation visible in your outward lifestyle and daily choices. He desires to change you from the inside out, and to use you in this life for His eternal purpose.

In short, you are special. Once you belong to God, He desires to set you apart, to sanctify you and use you by His Spirit. The biblical word *sanctify* means to make holy or pure—to consecrate.

You see, while all of our sins were paid for on the Cross, and positionally we stand righteous and forgiven before God, we still wake up every day and face a struggle with sin. In this struggle, God calls us to a holy life, and His Spirit desires to continually purify us. After you are saved, you are no longer who you used to be, and therefore your Heavenly Father doesn't want you to act like you used to act. Thankfully, He doesn't leave us alone in the quest for daily holiness and purity. His Holy Spirit lives within us, enabling the everyday process of sanctification.

> The Christian life is too hard for you to live alone.

In other words, the Holy Spirit doesn't stop working at salvation. His work continues every moment of every day in transforming us into the image of Jesus Christ (Romans 8:29).

Have you ever tried to change yourself? Have you ever begun a new year with a full list of resolutions that fell apart within the first few weeks? Let's face it, whether it's deep spiritual issues of anger or character, or more basic habits of daily personal discipline, truly changing ourselves is nearly impossible. Our best efforts usually end in failure and frustration. And for too many, the Christian life is no different.

Too many Christians fall into a trap of self-effort. They begin the Christian life by faith in Christ, but then assume the responsibility of self-change—trying to live the Christian life in their own power and effort. This is always a failing proposition. In Galatians 3:3, Paul asks new Christians this question, "Are ye so foolish? having begun in the Spirit, are ye now made perfect by the flesh?" They had fallen into the same trap. What began at salvation as a work of the Spirit, they tried to continue in their own strength and power.

The Christian life is too hard for you to live alone. It's beyond your capacity. It must be lived in dependency upon the Spirit, and it must be a supernatural work from within. Let's more closely examine this sanctifying work—how God goes about "setting you apart" to live a life well-pleasing to Him.

THE HOLY SPIRIT SEARCHES

First Corinthians 2:10–11 teaches, "But God hath revealed them unto us by his Spirit: for the Spirit searcheth all things, yea, the deep things of God. For what man knoweth the things of a man, save the spirit of man which is in him? even so the things of God knoweth no man, but the Spirit of God."

And in Psalm 139:23–24 we read, "Search me, O God, and know my heart: try me, and know my thoughts: And see if there be any wicked way in me, and lead me in the way everlasting."

God's Spirit knows us better than we can possibly know ourselves. He can reveal things to us about our hearts and our lives that we would otherwise never see.

Have you ever looked into one of those magnifying mirrors? What a horrible experience! As I get older, I don't even like what I see in a normal mirror, much less one that shows me every pore up close. And yet, seeing something up close lets you examine more clearly and maintain more exactly. For ladies who are meticulous about their skin or facial care, these mirrors are a powerful resource.

Living with the Holy Spirit inside of you can provide the same kind of experience on a spiritual level. He searches the heart and reveals things you never saw before. In essence, He uncovers flaws and imperfections that you never cared about so that He might purify and sanctify your heart and life.

THE HOLY SPIRIT CONVICTS

As we saw in the first chapter, one of the Holy Spirit's primary ministries is to reprove. The word *reprove* means to convict, refute, confute—generally with a suggestion of shame on the person convicted. It means to bring to the light, to expose; to find fault with, and to correct. And just as the Holy Spirit convicted you of your need for a Saviour, His convicting work goes on every day in your heart.

When allowed to freely work in your heart, the Holy Spirit will prick your conscience every time you do something wrong. I remember this being one of the defining changes in my life from the moment I trusted Christ as Saviour. Suddenly, it was as if I had an internal voice alarming me every time I sinned. Prior to salvation, doing wrong didn't bother me all that much. I wasn't sensitive to sin. But after salvation, something alerted and stirred my conscience every time. This was none other than the voice of the Holy Spirit bringing conviction and compelling me to turn from sin and make my heart right with my Heavenly Father.

> Conviction is God's early warning system and protection in your life after salvation.

Conviction is a privilege! It means that God is working in you. Conviction is a gift! It's the Holy Spirit of God warning you away from a path that will ultimately hurt you. It is God's early warning system and protection in your life after salvation.

From the earliest moments of your Christian walk, throughout the rest of your life, you must make the daily decision of how to handle the conviction of the Holy Spirit. You will either respond to it or reject it, surrender to it or silence it. Many harden their hearts, resist the conviction, and eventually come to the place of being past sensitivity. The Bible calls this hardness of heart a *seared conscience* (1 Timothy 4:2).

Every time you respond to the Holy Spirit's conviction, you invite Him to continue working in your life—to continue transforming you. But every time you resist or reject that conviction, your heart becomes calloused and less able to hear Him. Don't go down that road! Don't ever come to the place in life where you stop desiring and appreciating the conviction of the Holy Spirit in your heart.

THE HOLY SPIRIT TEACHES

In John 14, Jesus was about to be crucified, and He was preparing His disciples for not only the crucifixion, but also His resurrection and ascension to Heaven. He was preparing them to continue on, though He would not physically be with them. Understandably, this was hard for them to grasp. Throughout the chapter, Jesus tells them that after He departs, God will send the Holy Spirit, the Comforter, to be with them. He actually tells them it is "expedient"—better for them for Him to go away so that the Holy Spirit can come.

In John 14:26 Jesus said, "But the Comforter, which is the Holy Ghost, whom the Father will send in my name, he shall teach you all things, and bring all things to your remembrance, whatsoever I have said unto you." Again in John 16:13 Jesus said, "Howbeit when he, the Spirit of truth, is come, he will guide you into all truth: for he shall not speak of himself; but whatsoever he shall hear, that shall he speak: and he will shew you things to come."

Many years later, the Apostle John wrote of this same truth in 1 John 2:27, "But the anointing which ye have received of him abideth in you, and ye need not that any man teach you: but as the same anointing teacheth you of all things, and is truth, and is no lie, and even as it hath taught you, ye shall abide in him."

The Holy Spirit is a teacher. It is His responsibility to help you understand God's Word. And since He is searching you and convicting you, He knows exactly how to take the Word of God and perfectly apply it to your heart in ways that no human being ever could.

Often when I'm preaching, people in the congregation wonder how I "knew." At the door they ask, "Did my wife talk to you?" "Were you speaking directly to me?" or "How in the world did you know I was struggling with that?" For a new Christian, this can be a bit harrowing at first. It's a little unsettling to think that a preacher can somehow read your mind or intuitively know something so personal about your life.

The fact is, I don't have a clue about these personal situations, but the Holy Spirit does. I had prayed and studied God's Word to prepare a Bible message. It would be humanly impossible for me to personally apply every verse to the particular needs of each individual listener. But the Holy Spirit does exactly that. He takes the message and the verses, and by His convicting and searching power, He leads those believers through a personal teaching session right there in the pew. He always speaks much more personally on the inside than I could on the outside.

This is His work—He teaches. What an incredible thought! Living in your heart right now is a Teacher who desires to guide you into all truth. Every time you read your Bible, hear a message, listen to godly music, or enjoy sweet fellowship with Christian friends, you can be listening to His voice and understanding what He is teaching you. In every circumstance of life, you have a divine power in you seeking to reveal the truth to you.

THE HOLY SPIRIT REMINDS

Again, John 14:26 says, "But the Comforter, which is the Holy Ghost, whom the Father will send in my name, he shall teach you all things, and bring all things to your remembrance, whatsoever I have said unto you." Consider that phrase, "…bring all things to your remembrance."

He is your heavenly reminder. He prompts you to remember truth and to do right. His mission is to lead you moment by moment in the daily details of life, always applying the principles of Scripture to your present circumstances. When witnessing, He will bring verses to mind. When facing a tough decision, He will recall principles that apply. When needing wisdom and insight, He will remind you of biblical truths that will guide your steps.

One of my favorite things to say to our staff and church family is, "Obey every impulse of the Holy Spirit." It's a simple challenge, but easier said than done. Every day of your life, the Holy Spirit of God desires to prompt you and remind you of the little right things you should do along the way. It may be loving your spouse, nurturing your children, sharing Christ with a co-worker, or helping a neighbor. It may be encouraging your pastor, caring for a Christian, or sending a note of gratitude to a friend. He will seek to remind you to apply truth to every situation and to honor God in every daily decision.

THE HOLY SPIRIT ENLIGHTENS

We all have blind spots—things we can't see about the circumstances we are facing. We all have paradigms that cause our perspective to skew one direction over another. And we've all faced moments when we just didn't know what we needed to know.

God has many ways of dealing with such limitations—His Word, godly counsel, prayer, etc. One of them is His Holy Spirit. The Spirit's job is to enlighten us—to reveal to us what we need to know that we didn't know before. It's His ministry to show us the things that everybody else misses.

To the undiscerning viewer, a person who hears and listens to the Holy Spirit often just appears to be *lucky*. They seem to make right choices more often. They seem to see risk or danger before others see it. They understand things and connect dots that others entirely miss. In reality, the Holy Spirit is not a good luck charm or some mystical power, but in a very practical and unassuming way, He turns the lights on for us and brings us into those "Aha!" moments. Think about this verse again in this light.

John 16:13, "Howbeit when he, the Spirit of truth, is come, he will guide you into all truth: for he shall not speak of himself; but whatsoever he shall hear, that shall he speak: and he will shew you things to come." He will guide us into all truth. He will give us discernment and wisdom. He applies truth specifically in the moments we are facing and guides us with what to do.

What a great companion!

THE HOLY SPIRIT PRODUCES GROWTH

Galatians 5:22–23 teaches, "But the fruit of the Spirit is love, joy, peace, longsuffering, gentleness, goodness, faith, meekness, temperance: against such there is no law." We will examine these traits more closely in a coming chapter, but as a part of His sanctifying ministry, the Holy Spirit produces spiritual fruit that grows in my life.

This is where the personal life change produced by the Holy Spirit becomes visible and evident in my life. This is what will cause others around me to pause and say, "Something's different about you! What happened to you?"

The Holy Spirit desires to cultivate good qualities in your heart that show up in your life, your relationships, and your daily walk.

THE HOLY SPIRIT PRODUCES HOLINESS

A nineteenth century Scottish minister, Robert Murray McCheyne wrote these words to Dan Edwards, a young missionary about to go to the field, "In great measure according to the purity and perfections of the instrument, will be the success. It is not great talents God blesses so much as great likeness to [Christ] Jesus. A holy minister is an awful weapon in the hand of God."

Holiness is something that many Christians couldn't care less about. It's not even a word we often use in our modern vernacular. Many people think of holiness in terms of arrogance or piety, while others associate it with charismatic energy and sensationalism. It is neither. It's a practical word we should embrace as Christians.

Holiness is simply purity from sin. It is the defining attribute of God, and it is His ultimate goal for every one of His children. He not only desires for you to be saved from the penalty of sin, He desires you to be pure from the presence of sin in your daily life.

This is the pinnacle work of His sanctifying ministry—to lead you away from practicing sin on a daily basis.

The result of the work of the Holy Spirit in you will be that you are aware of sin, you deal with sin, and you live to avoid sin. This doesn't mean you will never sin. It means you will sin less and respond biblically before God when you do. (We will see this more closely in chapter six.)

Ephesians 5:8–9 says, "For ye were sometimes darkness, but now are ye light in the Lord: walk as children of light: (For the fruit of the Spirit is in all goodness and righteousness and truth)."

And 1 Corinthians 6:19–20 teaches us, "What? know ye not that your body is the temple of the Holy Ghost which is in you, which ye have of God, and ye are not your own? For ye are bought with a price: therefore glorify God in your body, and in your spirit, which are God's."

> Holiness is the defining attribute of God, and His ultimate goal for every believer.

On a practical level, the Holy Spirit will always create a more holy lifestyle. He will guide you into right choices and relationships and away from harmful entertainment and practices. He will help you be an effective steward in every area of life.

The sanctifying ministry of the Holy Spirit is phenomenal! It is life-transforming in every way. But it is vital that you remember it is a lifelong work. In Philippians 1:6 we read, "Being confident of this very thing, that he which hath begun a good work in you will perform it until the day of Jesus Christ." God began a good work in you by His Spirit, but it doesn't happen overnight. It will take the rest of your life. Frankly, this can be frustrating at times. I often wish I could speed up the work of God's Holy Spirit. I want to be more mature, more gracious, and more holy—right now! It's so easy to become impatient with God's internal work of grace. But this verse tells us to live confidently because God's work is progressing in us every day, whether we feel it or not.

You will be tempted to lose sight of the Holy Spirit's sanctifying work. You will tend to forget that your heart, like that Luxembourg memorial, is sacred ground for God's grace. You will be tempted to resist the work of the Holy Spirit and to remain in a life of sin and fleshly living, in spite of the fact that you are saved.

Don't fall into that trap. You are God's child. You are special, and God desires to do a great work in and through you. Live every moment in light of the sanctifying ministry that the Holy Spirit is performing in you, and thank God every day that you are not alone in figuring out life and trying to live the Christian life. You are His masterpiece in progress.

THREE

HIS STRENGTHENING MINISTRY

ave you ever run out of gas? Early in our ministry, Terrie and I had a car with a digital fuel gauge that told you how many miles you could go before you hit empty. At least, that's what it was supposed to do.

One afternoon we were taking a drive to the mountains and spending some time together. Terrie noticed that the fuel gauge was getting low, and she reminded me to stop and get gas. Confidently, I chided her a bit and said, "Nope, the gauge says we have forty-three miles left before empty. We're fine for a while."

That didn't comfort her. She still encouraged me to stop and fuel up, and I continued to trust the gauge. About thirty minutes later, the gauge was still reading fourteen miles to empty, when suddenly the car began to sputter and stall. I knew I was toast! I should have listened to my wife. Quietly, we drifted to the shoulder, miles from a gas station. We were out of gas, and I was in trouble.

It's one thing to run out of gas on a trip; it's another thing to run out of gas in life. Life just has a way of repeatedly bringing us to total spiritual, emotional, and physical depletion. Exhausted. Fatigued. Weary. Few things can bring you to the place of bad decisions like spiritual weariness. When you get weary in life, everything can be viewed negatively. Vince Lombardi said, "Fatigue makes cowards of us all." Weariness has a profoundly negative impact on your life and family.

Many times throughout my life and ministry, I've reached weariness—having expended everything I could in physical, emotional, and spiritual energy. Sometimes a trial or burden causes weariness. Other times it may be a hectic schedule, or the endless expectations of others. Other times it is the result of sin or a failure to walk with God.

It's easy to misunderstand such a season—to misdiagnose weariness. It affects your attitude and your outlook, and it appears to accurately reflect a change of heart. Weariness can lead you to believe that you actually *feel* differently about life and that you need some radical change to make life enjoyable again. It can cause you to question the most foundational and important things in your heart. Many are the stories of marital infidelity, family abuse, financial ruin, and spiritual reversal that flowed from bad decisions made during times of weariness. Simply put, when you're depleted, life stinks and everything bothers you. It's during times of depletion that you are the most agitated by your kids, the most frustrated with your spouse, and the least patient with circumstances beyond your control. These are also the times when you tend to be the least spiritual in your perspective.

Sometimes a good night's sleep can help, but that's primarily physical in nature. Usually weariness runs deeper than just physical rest. It requires a deeper rest, and beyond that, *restoration*—reviving the soul and spirit. It requires a renewal of strength of heart, a refreshing of courage and confidence.

> The Holy Spirit will meet you at your lowest point. He will lift you up, strengthen you, and set you on solid ground.

Christian, I want to warn you about weariness. It can destroy you. No matter how excited you are this moment about being a Christian and having the Holy Spirit in your life, you *will* come to a time when it seems that passion is gone forever. You will come to moments when you've lost any sense of motivation to live for Christ or to rely on His Spirit. It is inevitable. It happens to every Christian. And those who survive are those who understand the strengthening ministry of the Holy Spirit.

God knew, long before you and I did, that we would face these trying times. He knew that life would require more strength than we possess, that it would be overwhelming. While we like to pretend that we have life "under control," He understands that life is beyond our control.

Are you identifying with these words? Are you in the middle of a time of discouragement or emptiness? Are you depleted and questioning the things you have valued for so long? If so, take hope. You are not alone. And what you are experiencing is a season that you must travel through with the Holy Spirit's help. There's no need to fall away from faith, to begin making bad choices, or to despair. God promises to renew your strength if you will wait on Him (Isaiah 40:29–31).

The word *wait* in Isaiah 40:31 literally means to bind together in patience. The picture is that you must bind your life to God—cast yourself in complete dependence upon Him and patiently wait until He renews your strength. It's what He promises to do.

The Holy Spirit will meet you at your lowest point. He will lift you up, strengthen you, and set you on solid ground once again. Your weariness is not a surprise to God. He's already there, ready to sustain you and lead you through. Let's take a closer, more personal look at how the Holy Spirit desires to breathe the fresh wind of His strength into your life.

THE HOLY SPIRIT LEADS AND GUIDES

We've seen in John 14:26 that the Holy Spirit will "teach" us and "bring all things to your remembrance," and Romans 8:14 says, "For as many as are led by the Spirit of God, they are the sons of God." Think about that phrase, "led by the Spirit of God."

Most people are led and often misled by emotions, feelings, and desires. But when the Holy Spirit came into your life, you received a new internal leader. Emotions and desires often deceive us, but when the Holy Spirit arrives on the scene, emotions are meant to come to order and follow in step with God's leading.

This is significant. It means, as a Christian, you can finally be free from daily aimlessness and emotional instability. Think of the implications this could have on your heart, your relationships, your career—literally every aspect of life! When the Holy Spirit is leading and guiding, life becomes much more stable and truth oriented. While the storms of life rage, your heart can be anchored in the leading and guiding presence of God. No need to worry. Anxiety can take a vacation. Stress can dissipate. God is in control, and His Holy Spirit is navigating every moment.

On board a ship or aircraft, you will always find a navigator. He is the one person aware of the vessel's position at all times. He is responsible for planning the trip, advising of travel conditions, warning of hazards, and keeping accurate communications to and from the captain. The navigator is essential to any safe and prosperous voyage.

Before your salvation, you were journeying through this life without a navigator. You were literally flying blind and hopeless. Today, the Holy Spirit is your navigator. He intimately understands your journey from start to finish. He knows exactly where you are this moment and how that position relates to the rest of your journey. He is aware of every hazard. And He keeps open communications and transmissions to and from your Captain.

What an awesome promise we have in the Spirit's strengthening ministry! Wherever you are right now, whatever circumstances you face—trust your Navigator. Listen to His voice and let Him lead and guide you safely home.

THE HOLY SPIRIT ASSURES

Every person struggles with a certain amount of insecurity. It's human nature to want acceptance and affirmation. We often go to great lengths to fit in and be socially acceptable. Nobody likes to wonder where they stand with others. It's a most unsettling feeling.

It is our heart's deepest longing to be unconditionally loved and fully accepted. We know we don't measure up. We know we fall short. And yet our hearts crave the knowledge that God is truly on our side, in spite of sin and failures.

Let's face it—it's easy to love someone when they are good. Exceptional behavior is attractive. It's when you are loved *in spite* of yourself that you know the deepest love possible. And this is the love that God has offered us—complete acceptance, unconditional love, and eternal security.

One of the great strengthening ministries of the Holy Spirit is to assure us of where we stand with God. He reminds us that God is on our side and working all things for our good. He is present in us to remind us of our absolute acceptance by the Heavenly Father.

Think about Romans 8:15–16, "For ye have not received the spirit of bondage again to fear; but ye have received the Spirit of adoption, whereby we cry, Abba, Father. The Spirit itself beareth witness with our spirit, that we are the children of God." In this verse, the Spirit allows us to cry out to God and call Him "Abba." This word is the common Hebrew word for "Daddy" or "Da-da," and it's the first syllable a little baby in the Middle East learns how to say, "Abba-abba-abba."

The picture in this passage is that you are God's precious child. He views you the way a faithful father would see his infant. Though you are not perfect, though you have done nothing to earn His love, though you will often fail—He fully embraces and accepts you as His own.

I'm amazed how many Christians cannot accept the fact that God *likes* them. It's easy for us to know that God loves us, but to think that He actually *likes* us escapes our grasp. But it's true! You are His delight, and His Holy Spirit resides in you to provide the steady, calm assurance that you are held in His hand, secure in His love, and safe in His care.

The great preacher of the late nineteenth and early twentieth century, G. Campbell Morgan, was reading God's Word to a shut-in widow when he came to the verse stating: "Lo I am with you alway…." He paused, looked up, and asked, "Isn't that a wonderful promise?" The dear lady replied, "No—it's a wonderful *reality*!" His loving presence truly is a wonderful reality for those who choose not to neglect Him.

THE HOLY SPIRIT COMFORTS

I can't imagine anything more disconcerting than spending three years with Jesus—God in the flesh—only to be told that He needed to leave. Imagine walking the earth with Jesus. You've seen Him feed thousands from nearly nothing. He has chased away threatening storms by mere words. He has healed every kind of disease and physical malady. He has pulled money from the mouth of a fish. He has raised the dead—on several occasions. Let's face it. This is someone you would want to stick with! Who wouldn't want to be on His team? After several years of this, you'd be feeling pretty confident about life.

And after all of this, He sits everyone down and says, "I need to go away." What a devastating moment that must have been for the disciples. Their minds must have wrestled with confusion, wonder, questions, and concern. This was not in their version of the script. Their script had a kingdom and positions of honor, as well as the liberation of their nation. Their script said nothing about a trial, a flogging, or a death sentence—much less an ascension to Heaven. And in the middle of this mental and emotional confusion, read the words of Jesus to His disciples:

"And I will pray the Father, and he shall give you another Comforter, that he may abide with you for ever; Even the Spirit of truth; whom the world cannot receive, because it seeth him not, neither knoweth him: but ye know him; for he dwelleth with you, and shall be in you" (John 14:16–17).

"But because I have said these things unto you, sorrow hath filled your heart. Nevertheless I tell you the truth; It is expedient for you that I go away: for if I go not away, the Comforter will not come unto you; but if I depart, I will send him unto you" (John 16:6–7).

The Holy Spirit is the Comforter. The word *comforter* means intercessor, consoler, and advocate. The Holy Spirit is God in you, for you, on your side— breathing hope and comfort into your life.

> The Holy Spirit is God in you, for you, on your side— breathing hope and comfort into your life.

He is a transcendent companion who not only knows the journey, but comforts and consoles you through tough times.

God knew life would be hard. Being a Christian doesn't remove hardness, it only assures that you can survive it with grace, purpose, and even joy. Everybody's life is tough in some way, but how many people do you know who venture through tough stuff with absolute strength, peace, and courage? Most people in the world do everything possible to avoid tragedy, and when it comes, they fall to pieces. Sorrow for an unsaved soul is an absolutely hopeless and overwhelming experience. But for those who know the Holy Spirit, sorrow is but for a while, and God provides comfort and strength to get through it. Christians sorrow with hope, while unbelievers sorrow with no hope (1 Thessalonians 4:13).

In John 14:27 Jesus said, "Let not your heart be troubled, neither let it be afraid." Because of the Comforter, we can find refuge from fear and emotional turmoil. It is the ministry of the Holy Spirit to meet you in the depths of your difficulty and console you with His hope and grace.

Often in life, there's no one who can intimately understand the deepest cares of your heart. Some may sincerely and lovingly try, but for the depths of comfort our soul craves, human effort just falls short. Perhaps you can identify with Job who was completely overwhelmed—engulfed in sorrow—and had no man who knew how to properly comfort. He said in Job 16:2, "I have heard many such things: miserable comforters are ye all." The psalmist also experienced this in Psalm 69:20, "Reproach hath broken my heart;

and I am full of heaviness: and I looked for some to take pity, but there was none; and for comforters, but I found none."

People can't fill this void. If they could, the world wouldn't be so consumed with painkillers—emotional and spiritual. What's the point of alcohol, drugs, and illicit sexual relationships? They are painkillers. They take the raw sting off of the emptiness of a life without God. The painkillers don't fix anything; in fact, they make issues worse! But they provide temporary comfort: a momentary relief from the pains of the heart.

The Holy Spirit of God releases us from this prison. He rescues us from this endless search for temporary comfort, and He provides the true comfort for which your soul is searching. With the presence of the Holy Spirit, no child of God is ever without a resident Comforter. In the darkest moment of despair, if you turn to the Holy Spirit rather than painkillers, you will find Him eager to heal your heart and lead you through.

THE HOLY SPIRIT INTERCEDES

Have you ever been in the midst of such turmoil that you couldn't even find the presence of mind to pray with clarity? Some trials of life are so emotionally and mentally overwhelming that they leave us in a dense fog of reason and concern. These are times when you don't even know what you need, much less how to ask God for it. The circumstances have left you prayerful, but speechless.

Consider the ministry of intercession explained in Romans 8:26–27, "Likewise the Spirit also helpeth our infirmities: for we know not what we should pray for as we ought: but the Spirit itself maketh intercession for us with groanings which cannot be uttered. And he that searcheth the hearts knoweth what is the mind of the Spirit, because he maketh intercession for the saints according to the will of God." The Holy Spirit is your intercessor: He intervenes with the Heavenly Father for you. He knows your heart. He knows God's heart. He knows exactly what you need, and He bears you up before the Father with an intensity that the Bible describes as "groaning."

It's hard to imagine God the Spirit, from within your heart, crying out with groaning to God the Father, for you. What an amazing Comforter He is! He is an ever present helper—assisting, comforting, and interceding on your behalf.

THE HOLY SPIRIT GIVES PATIENCE AND HOPE

When life gets hard, our first prayer is usually something like, "God, make life easy again! Get me out of this!" That's a normal reaction, and understandable. But the Holy Spirit takes us beyond "normal." He lifts us beyond our capacity to see life through an entirely different lens. And this is where patience and hope come in.

Romans 15:13 teaches us that God wants us to abound in hope through the Holy Spirit, "Now the God of hope fill you with all joy and peace in believing, that ye may abound in hope, through the power of the Holy Ghost." And Romans 5:2–5 details the process of navigating tribulations by the Holy Spirit, "By whom also we have access by faith into this grace wherein we stand, and rejoice in hope of the glory of God. And not only so, but we glory in tribulations also: knowing that tribulation worketh patience; And patience, experience; and experience, hope: And hope maketh not ashamed; because the love of God is shed abroad in our hearts by the Holy Ghost which is given unto us."

Patience and hope—the divinely imparted ability to endure the trial (patience) and to see, by faith, the good hand of God through it (hope). This is supernatural strength (patience) and supernatural perspective (hope) coming from the Holy Spirit in your heart and converging upon your circumstances. It is not something that human nature can conjure up, and it doesn't come from the power of positive thinking. It comes only from the Holy Spirit of God, and it endures every trial with confident serenity and faith-filled optimism.

It has been said that "Faith cannot be developed in comfortable surroundings." God does something special in our lives through difficult times. Apart from God, the difficulties of life could be chalked up to fate—purposeless, pointless, and meaningless. But when you belong to Him, every dynamic of life has eternal implications. Every trial has a hopeful outcome and every hardship involves the hand of God working something for your good.

THE HOLY SPIRIT RENEWS STRENGTH

Runners have a term—*second wind*. Every long distance runner understands the phenomenon. A second wind happens when an athlete who is too weary to continue, unexpectedly finds a sudden surge or boost of energy to press on at peak performance. Medical experts believe the second wind is part physiological and part psychological. A second wind allows an athlete to perform beyond their expected capacity.

In the spiritual life, the Holy Spirit is your perpetual second wind. It is He who provides you with the strength to endure and the energy to press on at peak spiritual performance, even when you believe your strength is all but gone. In the marathon of the Christian life, when you've run long and hard, when your spirit is growing weary and you wonder how you will go another day—He runs to your side and breathes a second wind into your spiritual lungs.

The Bible says in Ephesians 3:16, "That he would grant you, according to the riches of his glory, to be strengthened with might by his Spirit in the inner man." We read in 2 Corinthians 4:16, "For which cause we faint not; but though our outward man perish, yet the inward man is renewed day by day."

One day at a time, one leg of the journey at a time, you can count on the fact that the Holy Spirit will renew your strength. He will provide exactly what you need to make it through today. And He will be there tomorrow to do the same.

Through all of the things mentioned in this chapter, the Holy Spirit gives strength. He is the secret source of every Christian. He *leads* and *guides* your life. He *assures* you of your standing with God. He *comforts* and *consoles* you through life's sorrows. He *intercedes* for you when you don't even know what to pray for. He provides *patience* and *hope*—supernatural endurance and perspective. And He *renews strength*—perpetually providing a second wind to ready-to-drop runners.

Are you relying upon Him? Are you acknowledging His presence? He is easily ignored. He won't force His strength upon you. Why not turn to Him right now? Talk with Him. Ask Him to renew your strength. Walk today in the wonderful presence of His strengthening ministry.

May you say with the psalmist, "My flesh and my heart faileth: but God is the strength of my heart, and my portion for ever" (Psalm 73:26).

HIS SERVING MINISTRY (PART ONE)

I n the summer of 2006, our church family surprised us with a trip to London for our twentieth anniversary. It had been a long-time dream of mine to visit Europe and study the heritage of our Christian faith. During the trip, we visited a place I will never forget—the burial ground of the non-conformists—Bunhill Fields located just north of the city of London. This was where faithful Christians from the 1600s–1800s were buried—those who refused to follow the Church of Rome or the Church of England. Many of these non-conformists, also known as dissenters, were Bible-believing Baptists who suffered horrific martyrs' deaths because they would not align with unbiblical practices and heretical church structures. Many of them willingly laid down their lives rather than give up their faith.

Walking through that cemetery was like walking through a sermon. It seemed every grave marker spoke to my heart—as if every Christian buried there said to me, "I laid my life down. What have you done for Jesus?"

Eventually, I came across the tombstone of John Rippon, a Baptist pastor in London in the late 1700s and early 1800s. His story is remarkable. He began serving the Lord at the age of seventeen, attending Bristol Baptist College in Bristol, England. About that same time he was called to pastor the Baptist Meeting House, which eventually became the legendary Metropolitan Tabernacle, the largest Baptist Church in England in that era, pastored by Charles Haddon Spurgeon.

During his life and ministry, John Rippon wrote such great hymns as "How Firm a Foundation" and "All Hail the Power of Jesus' Name," along with dozens of others. He personally published a hymnal that was printed twenty-seven times and sold over 200,000 copies.

His grave was not among the well-known at Westminster Abbey. He was not accepted among the religious elite of his day. He was scorned and labeled a dissenter, refusing to conform to the Church of England. But as a young man, the Holy Spirit of God compelled him to a simple and faithful life of service and surrender. He understood his call in life, and fully yielded himself to his Saviour. For sixty-three years he served Christ in the power of the Holy Spirit, and his legacy lives on to this day through the generations he touched and the hymns he wrote.

His grave marker and his story were a source of great conviction in my heart. It read as follows:

> The Rev. John Rippon, D.D., for 63 years pastor of a Baptist Church in Carter Lane, Southwark: as a man and as a minister, he was endeared to all who intimately knew him. His talents pre-eminently qualified him for the useful and acceptable discharge of his Public Duties. Affable in manner, affectionate in disposition, animated in the pulpit, in doctrine uncorrupt, unwavering in principle; his preaching was attractive, and his labours were abundant and successful. Among his varied services in the cause of religion, by none was he better known, or will be longer remembered in the Churches at home and abroad, than by the judicious and comprehensive Selection of Hymns bearing his name, which has aided the devotions and inspired the praises of myriads of his fellow Christians.

As I stood there in the non-conformists cemetery, the Holy Spirit ignited a greater passion in me to remain fully engaged in the cause of Christ, and to live my life on purpose for His high calling.

The only thing of value that will outlive your short life on this planet is the eternal purpose of God being fulfilled through your life. What are you doing that has eternal value? What is God accomplishing through you? In what eternal cause are you engaged?

One of the greatest ministries of the Holy Spirit is that He compels us to biblical service. He calls us out of aimless living and engages us in God's eternal cause. He stirs our hearts with a passion to do more than merely exist. He constantly presses the child of God to be active in the service of God Almighty.

Complacent Christians hide their faith in silence on the sidelines of service, but authentic Christianity is not designed for spectators. The Christian life is a call to action—to service. When the Holy Spirit took up residence in your life, He immediately desired to stir your heart and to place you into "active-duty" for God's purposes. I'm not saying that every believer is called to full-time, vocational ministry, but I am saying that every believer is called to serve God in some way. In fact, the Christian life is designed to be a life of not merely input or output but *throughput*. All of God's saving and strengthening resources that we have studied flow *into* you that they might flow *through* you to others. The Holy Spirit wants to make you a vessel through which He can bless others. You are to be a conduit, delivering the message of Christ and the gifts of God to the lives of others. You are to be His ambassador, divinely appointed and anointed by His Spirit—His servant to your family, your church family, your community, your workplace, and your world.

John Rippon grasped this before his seventeenth birthday, and I pray you will grasp it right now. The Holy Spirit wants to use you today!

Many Christians accept God's gift of *salvation*, and enjoy His ministry of *strengthening*, but never enter into the ministry of *service*. First Corinthians 3:9 says, "For we are labourers together with God…." It is wonderful to be saved. It is exceptional to be strengthened day by day. But from the moment of salvation, you were designed to *serve*. Believing-faith is exciting. Growing-faith is awesome. But serving-faith is indescribable! When the Holy Spirit engages you in eternal work, it takes your Christian life to the highest level of experience and value. Consider with me, the serving ministry of the Holy Spirit.

THE HOLY SPIRIT CALLS US

It's easy to live with no thought of a calling. Aimless and directionless, we tend to take life as it comes at us, reacting to events rather than engaging in a predetermined course. God designed you to do more than exist.

What gets you out of bed in the morning? What compels you forward? What inspires you and motivates you to live each day with clarity, direction, and purpose? Is your life in focus? The Holy Spirit's ministry is to clarify a very specific calling in your heart, that you might live each day on purpose with eternity in view.

In Acts 13:1–2, we read of this in the lives of Barnabas and Saul: "Now there were in the church that was at Antioch certain prophets and teachers; as Barnabas, and Simeon that was called Niger, and Lucius of Cyrene, and Manaen, which had been brought up with Herod the tetrarch, and Saul. As they ministered to the Lord, and fasted, the Holy Ghost said, Separate me Barnabas and Saul for the work whereunto I have called them."

In 2 Timothy 1:13–14, the Apostle Paul challenges Timothy to stay true to his calling which was given by the Holy Ghost— "Hold fast the form of sound words, which thou hast heard of me, in faith and love which is in Christ Jesus. That good thing which was committed unto thee keep by the Holy Ghost which dwelleth in us."

Finally, Ephesians 4:4 teaches us, "There is one body, and one Spirit, even as ye are called in one hope of your calling." From the moment of salvation, God's call on your life is real, and only His Holy Spirit can help you understand it and embrace it.

Some years ago I read of Captain Timothy Stackpole, a New York firefighter, who was severely burned in a 1998 fire. After months of rehabilitation, he insisted on returning to active duty in the late summer of 2001, and was shortly thereafter promoted to captain. Timothy was a great firefighter, and he was passionate about his work.

After his injury, many encouraged him to take a desk job rather than place himself in the front line of danger again. But Timothy flatly refused. Though he could have taken an easier assignment, his heart was committed to a cause. His answer—"You don't understand! I *have* to rescue people. It's my *duty*—it's my *calling!*"

On September 11, 2001, Timothy's shift had just ended and he was driving home from work when he heard the call for rescue workers to the World Trade Center. He immediately turned around and hurried to the Twin Towers where a horrific scene was unfolding. He quickly organized a group of rescuers and rushed into the number two tower to help people to safety. Moments later that tower collapsed, and Timothy Stackpole's life was taken.

He knew his calling—to save people—and he gave his life to fulfill that calling. Even so, the Holy Spirit of God has called you to a life of service. Few are called to *die* for Christ, but every Christian is called to *live* for Him.

Are you as clear about your calling as Timothy Stackpole was? Is your commitment as strong as his? The stakes are even higher. People within your reach are dying without Christ, and you hold the truths of salvation. You are called to help rescue them. You are called to share Christ with them.

THE HOLY SPIRIT EMPOWERS US

There's nothing more intimidating than taking on a responsibility in spiritual ministry. The stewardship of influencing others for Christ is tremendous. Thankfully, we don't have to depend upon ourselves in this work. Spiritual work requires spiritual resources, and the Holy Spirit is eager to empower us that we might be used beyond our capacity.

God's Word teaches that the Holy Spirit offers us His power as we engage in service. Throughout Scripture we read of God's Spirit coming upon people, filling them, and using them. History records stories of great revivals and spiritual awakenings brought on as humble, godly men became yielded vessels through which the power of God flowed.

Whether you are in full-time ministry or in a secular career field, the presence and call of the Holy Spirit in you makes you a prime candidate for the power of God. Think about it. Wouldn't you like God to touch and bless the simple details of your daily life for His purposes? Wouldn't you desire for Him to empower your words with greater influence, your witness with greater conviction and your life with greater effectiveness? Think of the eternal implications of the power of God at work through your life. This is not just for pastors or preachers. This is not just for those with some deep sense of purpose. This ministry of the Holy Spirit is for everyone who has received Christ. He wants to infuse the details of your daily life with the explosive power of God.

Jesus described it this way in Luke 4:18, "The Spirit of the Lord is upon me, because he hath anointed me to preach the gospel to the poor; he hath sent me to heal the brokenhearted, to preach deliverance to the captives, and recovering of sight to the blind, to set at liberty them that are bruised."

In Acts 1:4, Jesus actually commanded the disciples to "…wait for the promise of the Father…." He told them not to depart from Jerusalem until the Holy Spirit came upon them. Jesus would rather us not minister than attempt ministry in our own power! We must have the power of the Holy Spirit to accomplish anything of value to God.

John 20:21–22 says, "Then said Jesus to them again, Peace be unto you: as my Father hath sent me, even so send I you. And when he had said this, he breathed on them, and saith unto them, Receive ye the Holy Ghost." He said it also in John 15:5, "I am the vine, ye are the branches: He that abideth in me, and I in him, the same bringeth forth much fruit: for without me ye can do nothing." Apart from His power, our service is ineffective and pointless.

> The Holy Spirit is eager to empower us that we might be used beyond our capacity.

In Acts 1:8 we read this wonderful promise, "But ye shall receive power, after that the Holy Ghost is come upon you: and ye shall be witnesses unto me both in Jerusalem, and in all Judaea, and in Samaria, and unto the uttermost part of the earth." Think about it—you shall receive power, after the Holy Ghost is come upon you, to be witnesses—a certain promise, followed by a comforting presence, resulting in a converting power! In the book of Acts we see that the Holy Spirit wrought great things through the ministry of the early Christians who were essentially common people with an uncommon power upon their lives. Here are just a few examples:

> And when they had prayed, the place was shaken where they were assembled together; and they were all filled with the Holy Ghost, and they spake the word of God with boldness.—ACTS 4:31

> And with great power gave the apostles witness of the resurrection of the Lord Jesus: and great grace was upon them all.—ACTS 4:33

> And Stephen, full of faith and power, did great wonders and miracles among the people. —ACTS 6:8

> For he was a good man, and full of the Holy Ghost and of faith: and much people was added unto the Lord.—ACTS 11:24

> And the disciples were filled with joy, and with the Holy Ghost.—ACTS 13:52

These early Christians turned their world upside down (Acts 17:6). How? Certainly not in their own power, for they were poor, uneducated, simple men. God's power upon common men produces uncommon results—beyond-your-capacity results!

The thought of attempting God's work without God's power reminds me of a humorous story I read recently: Because of the trust he developed with many Arab tribes, the famous British scholar and soldier, "Lawrence of Arabia," participated in the Paris peace talks after World War I. Several Arab leaders came with him to Paris and stayed in the same hotel—a modern facility unlike anything they had ever seen before.

When they went into their bathrooms, they were astounded by the seemingly unlimited supply of water that would flow into the bathtub or sink by merely turning the faucet handles. They were so enamoured, that when preparing to leave Paris, they physically removed the faucet fixtures from the plumbing and packed them into their luggage, thinking that the faucets themselves magically created the vast amounts of water.

When they told Lawrence what they had done, he laughed and explained that the faucets were useless unless connected to pipes that were, in turn, connected to a source of water.

Many Christians are a lot like these Arab leaders—attempting to create spiritual results with nothing but the fixtures, and it's a hopeless effort. The fixtures must be firmly attached to the source! There are three ways we can attempt to do the work of God: we can trust our own strength and wisdom only to fail; we can borrow the resources of the world and manufacture artificial results; or we can depend on the power of God and see eternal results.

Nineteenth century preacher and revivalist Vance Havner wrote, "We say we depend on the Holy Spirit, but actually we are so wired up with our own devices that if the fire does not fall from heaven, we can turn on a switch and produce false fire of our own. If there is no sound of a rushing mighty wind, we have the furnace all set to blow hot air instead. God save us from a synthetic Pentecost!"

The late Dr. A. W. Tozer, author and pastor, said, "If the Holy Spirit was withdrawn from the church today, 95 percent of what we do would go on and no one would know the difference."

It's tragic that so few Christians truly live each day engaged in their calling and empowered by the Holy Spirit. Our natural bent is to live by the flesh, to please the flesh. We are dulled in our senses and passive toward God's purposes. It's tragic that so few Christians ever share their faith or lead someone else to Christ—that so few enjoy fulfilling the very purposes for which God created them.

> The Holy Spirit wants to infuse the details of your daily life with the explosive power of God.

Do you realize how quickly your life will pass? God's call and God's power await your embrace. Time is of the essence. This is not something to postpone or contemplate. I pray you will sense the urgency, and let the Holy Spirit focus your life priorities upon His call.

A young missionary named Herbert Jackson was given a car to help him in his work. The car was a major asset, but it had one difficulty—it would not start without a push or a jump-start. Jackson devised a system to cope with the car's inability to start. When he was ready to leave his home, he went to a nearby school and asked permission to bring some of the children out of class to help him push-start his car.

Throughout the day, he was careful to always park on a hill or to leave his engine running when he stopped for short visits. For two years the young missionary used what he believed was an ingenious method to enable him to use the car.

When poor health forced the Jackson family to leave the field, a new missionary arrived to lead the mission. When Jackson explained to the new missionary his methods for starting the car, the young man opened the hood and began inspecting. "Why, Dr. Jackson," he interrupted, "I believe the only trouble is this loose cable." He gave the cable a twist, pushed the switch, and the engine roared to life.

For two years, Dr. Jackson had used his own devices and endured needless trouble. The power to start the car was there all the time—it only needed to be connected.

Even so, in your life, the power of the Holy Spirit is in you— the power to be used of God awaits connection. One preacher appropriately said, "Anything done in our own strength will fail miserably, or succeed even more miserably."

The Holy Spirit's *call* and *empowering* are really just the beginning of the ways the Holy Spirit ministers through us in the service of Christ. In the next chapter, we'll learn even more specifically how the Holy Spirit places us into daily ministry.

FIVE

HIS SERVING MINISTRY (PART TWO)

T he Holy Spirit of God will lead you into the service of Christ. It's what He does! We've seen that He calls every believer, and He empowers every believer to perform His call. But there's much more to His serving ministry...

THE HOLY SPIRIT ENABLES US

If you don't feel inadequate for ministry, you are either prideful or delusional. The thought of actually serving God is terrifying for those who have never experienced His power in service. That first step into local church ministry, that first attempt to witness to a friend, that first day to sing in the choir, or that first day to teach a class can be a fearful experience. The devil does everything he can to intimidate us into silence and passivity—to sideline us. The last thing he wants is for you to begin serving God in the Spirit's power.

I love the quote, "With God's calling always comes God's enabling." Thousands of times I have looked around in ministry, and like Peter out on the water, I've been tempted to panic because I'm in so far over my head. All ministry is beyond us. Life change is bigger than human ability. The needs of people are beyond your capacity to meet. It's much easier to focus on the small stuff of life. The spiritual stuff scares us.

But that's the wrong perspective. When God calls you to do something, He not only promises to empower you, He also enables you. If He leads you to witness, He will give you the courage and the words to say. If He leads you to teach, He will enable you to communicate effectively. If He calls you to give, He will enable financial provision. God would never call you without enabling you and providing everything you need to get the job done.

I love how the Apostle Paul described his ministry in 1 Corinthians 2:3–5, "And I was with you in weakness, and in fear, and in much trembling. And my speech and my preaching was not with enticing words of man's wisdom, but in demonstration of the Spirit and of power: That your faith should not stand in the wisdom of men, but in the power of God."

In 2 Corinthians 4:7–10 he further described both his weakness and God's enabling power, "But we have this treasure in earthen vessels, that the excellency of the power may be of God, and not of us. We are troubled on every side, yet not distressed; we are perplexed, but not in despair; Persecuted, but not forsaken; cast down, but not destroyed; Always bearing about in the body the dying of the Lord Jesus, that the life also of Jesus might be made manifest in our body."

Do you see his human frailty and inability described in these verses? These words are coming from one of God's choice servants—a man who wrote much of the New Testament and took the Gospel to the known world of his day. His impact upon world history was profound, not because of himself, but because of God's enabling.

About the time you start to shrink away from ministry in fear and intimidation, let the Holy Spirit remind you of these verses—2 Timothy 1:7–8, "For God hath not given us the spirit of fear; but of power, and of love, and of a sound mind. Be not thou therefore ashamed of the testimony of our Lord, nor of me his prisoner: but be thou partaker of the afflictions of the gospel according to the power of God."

Corrie ten Boom rightly wrote, "Trying to do the Lord's work in your own strength is the most confusing, exhausting, and tedious of all work. But when you are filled with the Holy Spirit, then the ministry of Jesus just flows out of you." What a great way to describe His power and His ability flowing through you.

Allowing God to empower and enable you for His service is one of the most rewarding experiences of the Christian life.

THE HOLY SPIRIT GIVES BOLDNESS

In the book of Acts, first century Christians had uncommon boldness—the ability to be courageously outspoken with great confidence and assurance. What a great quality! Look at how the Holy Spirit created this in Acts 4:31, "And when they had prayed, the place was shaken where they were assembled together; and they were all filled with the Holy Ghost, and they spake the word of God with boldness."

Timidity is not a gift of the Holy Spirit. Quite the opposite. The Spirit of God is compelling. He will not stay silent when truth should be proclaimed. In the face of rejection, scorn, and even torture, Christians in the first century were bold to speak God's Word.

In great contrast, many today limit the Holy Spirit to quiet, non-confrontational types of community service. While these may have social value, the Holy Spirit will always compel the believer out of silence to speak the truth in the love of Christ. He will give you the will, the capacity, and the courage to speak up when speaking up is difficult or even risky. He will give you a holy boldness to stand up and speak truth when others would advise you to duck.

THE HOLY SPIRIT ENGAGES US

Perhaps by now you're thinking, "I realize I'm called, I want God's power, and I'm sensing a new courage from the Holy Spirit—but for what? How do I know specifically what to do?" This is where the compelling nature of the Holy Spirit becomes very personal. He engages us in God's work.

God has a mission for you to accomplish, and He intends to make that mission clear. He has a specific place where He intends to plug you into His work, and it's the work of His Holy Spirit to make the details of what you are to do very clear so you can obey Him.

Look at how the Holy Spirit directed and engaged Philip in this passage: "And the angel of the Lord spake unto Philip, saying, Arise, and go toward the south unto the way that goeth down from Jerusalem unto Gaza, which is desert. And he arose and went: and, behold, a man of Ethiopia, an eunuch of great authority under Candace queen of the Ethiopians, who had the charge of all her treasure, and had come to Jerusalem for to worship, Was returning, and sitting in his chariot read Esaias the prophet. Then the Spirit said unto Philip, Go near, and join thyself to this chariot" (Acts 8:26–29).

The Holy Spirit distinctly directed Philip to a particular location, at an exact time, for the express purpose of meeting a searching man in a chariot.

Here's another example. Notice how the Apostle Paul describes what the Spirit was directing him to do: "And now, behold, I go bound in the spirit unto Jerusalem, not knowing the things that shall befall me there: Save that the Holy Ghost witnesseth in every city, saying that bonds and afflictions abide me" (Acts 20:22–23). In this case, Paul described being "bound in the spirit." The leadership of the Holy Spirit was so clear, so compelling, so engaging, that Paul knew he *must* obey and follow.

In the early ministry of Jesus we read in Mark 1:12, "And immediately the Spirit driveth him into the wilderness."

These verses do not imply that free will is removed from the matter and the Holy Spirit holds us hostage. It describes a clarity so strong and a compulsion so powerful that the only other choice is to flatly and directly disobey.

One of the many times this has happened to me was in June of 1986. Our family was enjoying a vacation in Southern California and preparing to drive north to the beautiful national parks in the Sierras. As part of the trip, I had committed to a pastor in Lancaster to preach for his small congregation.

Driving into town I remember thinking I would never want to live in Lancaster. It was a small desert town an hour northeast of Los Angeles—a town near Edwards Air Force Base with a rich aerospace history, but little else! My plan was to preach and move on north to continue our vacation.

To our surprise, after the message that day, the congregation of a dozen or so actually voted to call me to be their pastor. My friend was preparing to leave for the mission field, and this little church needed a new pastor. To be honest, I didn't even pray about it. I just said "no." I had no intention of ever coming to this desert place called the Antelope Valley.

But something happened the next day that I wasn't expecting. That morning as we loaded up our car and began to leave Lancaster, the Holy Spirit started to compel my heart. It seemed at every corner I saw signs for new housing tracts and the Holy Spirit said, "I'm bringing a lot of families to this area—who will reach them for Christ?" At first I denied and even argued a bit. I thought, "This place is hot. This isn't what I was picturing in pastoring a church. I don't really want to live in a desert." But the Holy Spirit was relentlessly speaking to my heart. There was no doubt in my mind that He was "binding me" or "driving me"—compelling me to come to Lancaster, California.

The drive was very quiet that morning. I was wrestling with the Spirit, and my wife Terrie wasn't saying much either. After a time, I turned to her and said, "Honey, I think the Lord wants us to move to Lancaster…." And before I even finished my sentence, she said, "I do too…." As she spoke, I became aware that the Holy Spirit was doing the same exact work in her heart that He was doing in mine.

He was *engaging* us in a very specific time and place for a very specific work. We didn't need to wonder what God was compelling us to do—we only needed to obey. Isn't that interesting? Our greatest struggle with God's will isn't knowing what it is—it is obeying what we already know. It's the Holy Spirit's job to communicate clearly what God's will is, and then it's up to us to make the choice to obey.

THE HOLY SPIRIT UNIFIES US

There are a couple more stops on our discovery of the Holy Spirit's serving ministry. Yes, He calls us, empowers us, enables us, emboldens us, and engages us, but He doesn't lead us to work alone. God's pattern for His work is that His people serve together. He leads teams of believers to cooperate, in His Spirit, for His purposes.

The New Testament term for those "teams of believers" is *church*, and throughout the New Testament God established local churches—called-out assemblies of believers—and He worked in and through those churches to impact the entire world with the truth. It's impossible to honestly approach the New Testament pattern of ministry and exclude the local church. Jesus established the church, and He still works through local, called out assemblies of Bible believers all over the world.

Many today want to universalize the church—taking away its local nature and presuming it to be nothing more than a mystical conglomerate of believers all over the world. But in practical, everyday reality, the churches of the New Testament were real, local bodies in various cities, assembling together, laboring together, and reaching their cities together.

Popular authors and researchers today want to tell us that these types of churches are no longer effective. In their opinion, the concept of church has failed, society has moved beyond local churches, and Christians need to reinvent a more relevant model.

> Our greatest struggle with God's will isn't knowing what it is—it is obeying what we already know.

While I believe that denominations have certainly failed, and many so-called churches are irrelevant and flawed in their doctrine and practice, I must side with Jesus against the research. His model of local assemblies of faithful believers growing and serving together is still alive and well—and it works! All over the world I visit these churches and rejoice that the Spirit of Christ is still unifying believers around His truth and His purposes.

When the Holy Spirit engages you in service, He is going to do so in conjunction with and in the context of local church ministry.

Luigi Galvani was an Italian scientist in the late 1700s. He was one of the first men to ever venture into the field of bio-electricity, when in 1771, he discovered that a spark would cause the leg muscles in a dead frog to twitch and move. His name and his research led to the term *galvanization.*

Galvanization is a an electrochemical method of adhering a protective metal layer to another metal with the use of electrical current. The procedure is repeated, and the outcome is that the final metal, by being energized and joined together, is stronger, more protected, and more useful.

When it comes to the unifying ministry of the Holy Spirit, He wants to *galvanize* you—to move you into action with other believers, and to protect you through the accountability and strength of a local church body.

Notice what God says about this process:

> *Endeavouring to keep the unity of the Spirit in the bond of peace. There is one body, and one Spirit, even as ye are called in one hope of your calling; One Lord, one faith, one baptism, One God and Father of all, who is above all, and through all, and in you all.*—EPHESIANS 4:3–6

> *Now I beseech you, brethren, for the Lord Jesus Christ's sake, and for the love of the Spirit, that ye strive together with me in your prayers to God for me.*—ROMANS 15:30

Only let your conversation be as it becometh the
gospel of Christ: that whether I come and see you, or
else be absent, I may hear of your affairs, that ye stand
fast in one spirit, with one mind striving together for
the faith of the gospel;—PHILIPPIANS 1:27

Over and over, He commands us to let the Holy Spirit bring us into unity and cooperation with other believers. And all of the admonitions above were given to local churches.

Interestingly, these same principles apply in the home as well. No home or church can survive without the unifying ministry of the Spirit. He is the secret of harmony among human hearts. Warren Weirsbe said, "It is power from within, not pressure from without that holds the church and the home together."

When it comes to God's work and seeing God do something great by His Spirit, unity is necessary. A.W. Tozer used the following metaphor to illustrate the importance of unity:

"You may have electricity supplied to your home, but if your walls have broken wiring, the electrical fixtures won't work. The lights won't turn on and the appliances won't work unless the wiring is connected properly to the power source. The power may be available and ready to do its work, but broken wiring will render the power useless. Unity is necessary among the children of God if we are going to know the flow of power—to see God do His wonders."

Notice what God did in Acts 4:31–32 when believers were praying and serving in unity, "And when they had prayed, the place was shaken where they were assembled together; and they were all filled with the Holy Ghost, and they spake the word of God with boldness. And the multitude of them that believed were of one heart and of one soul: neither said any of them that ought of the things which he possessed was his own; but they had all things common."

Hear the Holy Spirit's plea for unity with fellow believers in Philippians 2:1–3, "If there be therefore any consolation in Christ, if any comfort of love, if any fellowship of the Spirit, if any bowels and mercies, Fulfil ye my joy, that ye be likeminded, having the same love, being of one accord, of one mind. Let nothing be done through strife or vainglory; but in lowliness of mind let each esteem other better than themselves."

When the Holy Spirit is working in your life, He will help you set aside pettiness, gossip, and strife. He will help you put away your own agenda and personal preferences, and He will create in you a desire for humble cooperation and unity with your local church family for the sake of the Gospel.

THE HOLY SPIRIT EXALTS CHRIST

For what purpose does the Holy Spirit call us, empower us, enable us, embolden us, engage us, and unify us? It's all about Jesus. His primary ministry is to uplift and magnify the Lord Jesus Christ. John 15:26 says, "But when the Comforter is come, whom I will send unto you from the Father, even the Spirit of truth, which proceedeth from the Father, he shall testify of me." Again we see it in John 16:14, "He shall glorify me…."

> "But we have this treasure in earthen vessels, that the excellency of the power may be of God, and not of us."—2 Corinthians 4:7

Notice 1 Corinthians 12:3, "Wherefore I give you to understand, that no man speaking by the Spirit of God calleth Jesus accursed: and that no man can say that Jesus is the Lord, but by the Holy Ghost."

Why would God use you or me? We are but earthen vessels. What is man that He would be mindful of us? We are nothing but dust. What an overwhelming thought that God desires to magnify His Son through us.

This happened in Acts 4:13, "Now when they saw the boldness of Peter and John, and perceived that they were unlearned and ignorant men, they marvelled; and they took knowledge of them, that they had been with Jesus." And God describes it again in 2 Corinthians 4:7, "But we have this treasure in earthen vessels, that the excellency of the power may be of God, and not of us."

True, you and I are nothing. We are vessels of clay with nothing of ourselves to offer God. But when you were saved, His Holy Spirit came into your life and began a magnificent work. He desires to transform you and then to engage you in service. He desires for that service to be so power-filled and supernatural, so evidently "more-than-human" and beyond your capacity that people can only reasonably come to one conclusion—this must be of God. This must be about Jesus!

I will never forget my walk through the non-conformists cemetery in London. Walking past those tombstones was a vivid reminder of how many have gone before me in the service of Christ. My passion is to be like John Rippon, who at seventeen years of age, began a sixty-three year journey of faithful service for Jesus Christ. As a very young man, he understood that his short life on this planet was not about himself. It was about his Saviour. He heard the *call* of the Spirit. He claimed the *power* of the Spirit. He trusted the *enabling* of the Spirit. He experienced the *boldness* of the Spirit. He was *engaged* in specific service by the Spirit. He was *unified* with other believers in the Spirit. And he spent his life letting the Spirit *exalt Christ* through him. Here we are, nearly two hundred years later, contemplating the difference that his life made.

The only life worth living is the one that follows the Holy Spirit in the service of Jesus Christ. John Rippon understood that. Will you?

PART TWO
THE SPIRIT-FILLED LIFE

WHAT DOES IT MEAN TO BE SPIRIT-FILLED?

WHAT IS THE DAILY BATTLE?

HOW CAN THE BATTLE BE WON?

The Holy Spirit desires to bring
His full ministry and power into your daily life.
A Spirit-filled life is an incomparable life.
Truly it is a life beyond human capacity!

THE STRUGGLE
OF THE SPIRIT

On January 15, 2009, Captain Chesley Sullenberger began what, for him, was a normal workday—doing preflight preparations in the cockpit of an Airbus A320. He was assigned to US Airways flight 1549 from New York's LaGuardia airport bound for Charlotte, North Carolina. Shortly after 3:00 PM, 155 people were on board and ready for takeoff. It was all routine for Sullenberger, who had 42 years of flying experience.

Shortly after takeoff, while ascending over Manhattan, the plane unexpectedly hit a large flock of birds, causing both engines to completely lose thrust. One engine caught fire. With the plane disabled, Captain Sullenberger immediately began communicating with the control tower—his mind racing through options for how to land this plane safely with no engines. Returning to LaGuardia was not an option. There were no other airports or runways within range. It quickly became clear that his only option was to attempt to safely ditch the plane in the Hudson River along Manhattan's west side. He described the emotion of that moment as "the worst sickening, pit-of-your-stomach, falling-through-the-floor feeling" that he had ever experienced.

For several extremely quiet and tense moments, Sullenberger and his co-pilot called on all of their collective experience and knowledge to glide the Airbus A320 toward the Hudson. The lives of 155 people hung on the accuracy of every decision—a thousand factors had to come perfectly together in order to avoid tragedy.

Just before 3:30 PM, Sullenberger announced over the speaker system, "Brace for impact." A few moments later, the plane glided safely into the Hudson River, narrowly avoiding disaster. All 155 people onboard were safe. Ferries and rescue boats quickly met the sinking plane as passengers stood single-file on the wings. Sullenberger walked the length of the entire cabin twice, even as water rose above his waist, to make sure every passenger and crew member was evacuated.

The story of Sullenberger's heroic efforts and unusual calm throughout the incident captivated the entire world. When faced with probable calamity, he responded with improbable poise. When most would have panicked or overreacted, this man remained focused, composed, and resolved. Speaking in an interview after the incident, he said, "One way of looking at this might be that for forty-two years, I've been making small, regular deposits in this bank of experience, education, and training. And on January 15, the balance was sufficient so that I could make a very large withdrawal."

I can't imagine the internal struggle that Captain Sullenberger faced in bringing that aircraft to rest on the Hudson River. While every human emotion would have been screaming at him to fear, to panic, and to react hastily, with quiet strength he chose to call on forty-two years of experience. With absolute focus, ignoring his natural responses, he maintained composure and control.

The day you trusted Christ and the Holy Spirit came into your life, you began a similar struggle. As a child of God, you were given a new nature by His Spirit. The Holy Spirit brought into your life a new set of desires, a new creature with all the potential to live a holy and godly life. Your old nature—the "old man" as the Bible refers to it—was crucified with Christ. In other words, the source of your sinfulness was done away with, and you were given a new nature with good desires through the Spirit.

In this light, it seems as though the struggle against sin would have been utterly done away with at salvation. But this isn't the case. The plot thickens a bit here. While your old nature has been replaced by a new nature, you still live in the flesh, and this is where the real struggle of the Christian life resides—the flesh against the Spirit. You now live every day with a new heart and a new nature struggling against a well-programmed sinful flesh—a brain, a body, and physical impulses that are well ingrained with sinful patterns of behavior. In your new nature, because of the ministry of the Holy Spirit, you have a new set of desires—desires to please God, to live for Him, to avoid sin, and to lead a righteous life. But in your flesh resides the power of sin wrestling for control and demanding submission. While the Spirit convicts and creates a thirst for righteousness, the flesh fights to have its own way and to draw you back into sin. In spite of the fact that your old nature has been crucified, it is entirely possible to live in the flesh—to live as though the old man is alive and well. The Bible refers to this as being "carnal." (1 Corinthians 3:1, "And I, brethren, could not speak unto you as unto spiritual, but as unto carnal, even as unto babes in Christ.")

Frankly, this struggle is the most frustrating experience of the Christian life. It will plague you for the rest of your natural life, but in the midst of the struggle, there is hope, a path to victory, and eventually, complete deliverance. Remember, the Holy Spirit is the power and presence of God in you. He can win the struggle, but it all comes down to your daily choices. Let's examine this struggle more closely. For if you don't understand it, you will no doubt become frustrated and quit altogether. The devil would love for you to believe that you just can't win. He would love to have you think that your old nature is still alive and that you really have no hope of real transformation. But that's not the case.

THE STRUGGLE WITH THE FLESH

The Apostle Paul referred to this struggle in Romans. Let's take a close look at Romans 7:15–25:

For that which I do I allow not: for what I would, that do I not; but what I hate, that do I. If then I do that which I would not, I consent unto the law that it is good. Now then it is no more I that do it, but sin that dwelleth in me. For I know that in me (that is, in my flesh,) dwelleth no good thing: for to will is present with me; but how to perform that which is good I find not. For the good that I would I do not: but the evil which I would not, that I do. Now if I do that I would not, it is no more I that do it, but sin that dwelleth in me. I find then a law, that, when I would do good, evil is present with me. For I delight in the law of God after the inward man: But I see another law in my members, warring against the law of my mind, and bringing me into captivity to the law of sin which is in my members. O wretched man that I am! who shall deliver me from the body of this death? I thank God through Jesus Christ our Lord. So then with the mind I myself serve the law of God; but with the flesh the law of sin.

After reading that, you could almost conclude that Paul was confused. On one hand he speaks of his good desires, and on the other his bad performance of those desires. He makes it very clear that his heart has been implanted with the will to do good—that's the work of the Spirit. But he also makes it clear that he struggles with bringing those good intentions to reality.

Several times he makes a very important distinction when it comes to sin. He says, "…it is no more I that do it, but sin that dwelleth in me." This is not blame shifting—it's truth. And it's a very important truth for you to grasp. Paul was saying, "The real me—the new me—desires to do good, but the power of sin in me still fights against the performance of good." He makes a powerful case that the heart—the inward man—can delight in the laws of God, while the power of sin in his "members" (or his body) wars against the laws of God.

Do you get this picture? After salvation, you are a new creature living in an old body. You are a new nature dwelling in a sinful flesh. The two fight for control of your life every single day. We read it again in Galatians 5:17, "For the flesh lusteth against the Spirit, and the Spirit against the flesh: and these are contrary the one to the other: so that ye cannot do the things that ye would."

It's important that you understand the difference between having a new nature and having a sin nature because if it is your nature to sin, you are doomed to failure. But if it is your nature to do good, then through the power of God, that new nature can overcome the fleshly habits. Let me illustrate.

You are not a dog. But you could *believe* you are a dog. And in so believing, you could act like a dog. For instance, you could bark. You could crawl around on all fours. You could eat out of a dish on the floor. And you could expect people to pat you on the head. None of this would make you a dog. No matter what you do, you could never be a dog. But you could be a person acting like a dog.

Here's the real catch. If you believe you are a dog, then your actions will follow your belief.

So it is in the Christian life. If you believe you have a sin nature, then your behavior will follow that belief. You will believe you are essentially stuck in sin. You will reason, "This is just the way I am." In Christian growth, you will never move beyond your belief. If you believe you are a dog, then you will act like a dog.

> In Christian growth, you will never move beyond your belief.

This is why the Bible teaches that you are a new creature. Indeed, you received a new nature at salvation. We're not talking about a clean up job or a reforming job of the old nature. We're talking about a *crucifixion*—death to the old nature—and *regeneration*—a new nature being born. This is the work of regeneration that we studied earlier. (Romans 6:6, "Knowing this, that our old man is crucified with him, that the body of sin might be destroyed....")

The first step to real growth in the Holy Spirit, and to spiritual victory over the flesh is to believe what God says about your new nature—the new man. Ephesians 4:24 says, "And that ye put on the new man, which after God is created in righteousness and true holiness." Second Corinthians 5:17 says, "Therefore if any man be in Christ, he is a new creature: old things are passed away; behold, all things are become new."

The second step to victory is to daily "put off" the old man and "put on" the new man—to "put on Christ" just as you put on a clean set of clothes every morning. Ephesians 4:22, "That ye put off concerning the former conversation the old man, which is corrupt according to the deceitful lusts." Colossians 3:10, "And have put on the new man, which is renewed in knowledge after the image of him that created him." Galatians 3:27, "For as many of you as have been baptized into Christ have put on Christ." This is also addressed in Romans 12:2, "And be not conformed to this world: but be ye transformed by the renewing of your mind, that ye may prove what is that good, and acceptable, and perfect, will of God." We will study this principle more in chapter twelve.

Each day, you will face the struggle of the flesh against the Spirit, and each day you will make a decision to either put on the new man or to walk in the ways of the old man.

REBIRTH, RENEWAL, REDEMPTION

Another way to look at these principles in "big picture" form is by understanding God's three-part process in the work of eternal salvation. The moment you trusted Christ, a lot happened, and a lot began to happen. While salvation is a one-step decision, God has ordained a three-fold process in the complete work of redemption. Understanding this process is important to understanding the daily struggle of the Spirit in your life. It breaks down like this:

REBIRTH IS IMMEDIATE AT SALVATION

Rebirth was the miracle in the moment of decision—your spirit was made new and the Holy Spirit came into your heart.

> *Jesus answered and said unto him, Verily, verily, I say unto thee, Except a man be born again, he cannot see the kingdom of God.*—JOHN 3:3

> *…Verily, verily, I say unto thee, Except a man be born of water and of the Spirit, he cannot enter into the kingdom of God."*—JOHN 3:5

RENEWAL IS A LIFELONG, DAILY PROCESS

Renewal is the process of a lifetime. This is sanctification whereby God transforms my heart and life from the inside out.

> *And be not conformed to this world: but be ye transformed by the renewing of your mind, that ye*

> *may prove what is that good, and acceptable, and*
> *perfect, will of God.*—ROMANS 12:2

> *And be renewed in the spirit of your mind;*
> —EPHESIANS 4:23

> *For which cause we faint not; but though our outward*
> *man perish, yet the inward man is renewed day by*
> *day.*—2 CORINTHIANS 4:16

> *And have put on the new man, which is renewed*
> *in knowledge after the image of him that created*
> *him:*—COLOSSIANS 3:10

REDEMPTION IS A FUTURE PROMISE

Redemption is the final step of salvation when my sinful flesh will be traded in for a new body—a perfect body without sinful tendencies. This won't happen until we see the Lord at the end of this life.

> *And not only they, but ourselves also, which have*
> *the firstfruits of the Spirit, even we ourselves groan*
> *within ourselves, waiting for the adoption, to wit,*
> *the redemption of our body.*—ROMANS 8:23

> *For we know that if our earthly house of this*
> *tabernacle were dissolved, we have a building of*
> *God, an house not made with hands, eternal in the*

heavens. For in this we groan, earnestly desiring to be clothed upon with our house which is from heaven: If so be that being clothed we shall not be found naked. For we that are in this tabernacle do groan, being burdened: not for that we would be unclothed, but clothed upon, that mortality might be swallowed up of life. Now he that hath wrought us for the selfsame thing is God, who also hath given unto us the earnest of the Spirit.—2 CORINTHIANS 5:1–5

Which is the earnest of our inheritance until the redemption of the purchased possession, unto the praise of his glory.—EPHESIANS 1:14

Why does this matter? Because, until your body is redeemed, you will be undergoing God's good work of renewal and transformation—the renewing of your mind. With every passing day, the Holy Spirit desires to live out the character of Jesus Christ through your mind and body. This is the daily battle of the Christian life, and God designed it purposefully this way.

The struggle portrayed in Romans 7 is often frustrating, but God chose the process. He chose to glorify Himself through the daily transformation of your life. And while the struggle is at times discouraging, the victory is promised.

Paul didn't end Romans 7 in despair. In verse 24 he cries out, "O wretched man that I am! who shall deliver me from the body of this death?" Sounds pretty frustrated doesn't he? But then he quickly answers his own question in verse 25, "I thank God through Jesus Christ our Lord...." Then he proceeds in chapter 8 to describe the awesome, victorious life of allowing God to bring the flesh into the control of His Holy Spirit. We will take a closer look at that passage in chapter twelve.

> Each day you will make a decision to either put on the new man or to walk in the ways of the old man.

Years ago, an Indian chief would often gather his tribal warriors into a circle. He would place two fighting dogs in their midst, and every time, he would accurately predict which dog would win the fight. This would amaze the warriors.

One man said, "You are so wise. How is it that you always know which dog will be the winner?"

The chief said, "It is very easy. It depends on which one I feed the most before the fight."

The struggle of the flesh against the Spirit is very real. It rages every day in your life. Which one are you feeding the most? Is your flesh growing stronger every day through the appetites you feed, the thoughts you entertain, and the habits you continue? Or are you starving the flesh and feeding your spirit through spiritual resources? Are you filling your heart with the Word of God, spiritual music, strengthening fellowship, and Bible teaching?

If you are ignoring God's Holy Spirit and feeding the flesh, you will continually lose the struggle. But if you yield to the Spirit, and starve the flesh, you will win more and more with every passing day.

Chesley Sullenberger spent forty-two years preparing for the struggle of his life—a few extremely tense moments when his decisions held the fate of 155 people. The preparation paid off. When the struggle between his natural impulses and his years of experience collided, experience won. His years of deposits were worth every moment.

And so it is in your Christian life. If the struggle between the flesh and the Spirit will ever be won by the Spirit, you're going to have to make deposits into His account every day. You're going to have to yield to Him thousands upon thousands of times as He daily performs His renewing work. And over time, the wonderful life of Christ will begin to flow out of you—naturally. Good things will grow in your life and harvest time will come. The struggle of the Spirit, when handled properly, will victoriously bring forth wonderful fruit. That's the refreshing discovery of our next few chapters.

SEVEN

THE SWORD
OF THE SPIRIT

W hen a preacher's car broke down on a country road, he walked to a nearby roadhouse to use the phone. After calling for a tow truck, he spotted his old friend, Frank, drunk and shabbily dressed, staggering out of a bar. "What happened to you, Frank?" asked the good pastor. "You used to be rich."

Frank told a sad tale of bad investments and bad habits that had led to his downfall. "Go home," the preacher said. "Open your Bible at random; stick your finger on the page, and there will be God's answer."

Some time later, the preacher bumped into Frank, who was wearing a Gucci suit, sporting a Rolex watch, and stepping out of a

Mercedes Benz. "Frank," said the preacher, "I am glad to see things have turned around for you."

"Yes, Preacher, and I owe it all to you," said Frank. "I went home, opened my Bible, put my finger down on the page, and there was the answer—chapter 11!"

I think Frank may have been misguided in his idea of how God intends to use His Word in our lives. If you're truly going to discover how to live beyond your capacity by God's Spirit, the Bible is central. It is His primary weapon in winning the daily battle we just studied.

THE POWERFUL SWORD OF THE SPIRIT

Ephesians 6:17 teaches us, "And take the helmet of salvation, and the sword of the Spirit, which is the word of God." The Word of God is a sword in the Spirit's hands. The word *sword* refers to a weapon of war. The sword would have been a powerful metaphor for the Christians at Ephesus when they received this letter from the Apostle Paul. They would have seen swords often in the possession of Roman centurions who were ruling the region of the Roman Empire. History records some interesting facts about the *gladius* (the Latin word for the sword of the Roman soldier):

The sword is a symbol of power and authority. It was carried by those in authority and held the weight of justice and rule. It was a symbol of power and strength. Even so, the Word of God is powerful, and it represents the authority and strength of Almighty God. It is the highest authority with which we can enter spiritual battle.

Hebrews 1:3 speaks of Jesus and the power of God's Word, "Who being the brightness of his glory, and the express image of his person, and upholding all things by the word of his power, when he had by himself purged our sins, sat down on the right hand of the Majesty on high."

The sword is an offensive weapon. It was to be used to attack an enemy and to penetrate opposition. It was not designed for retreat, but for engagement. Likewise, the Word of God is to be used as an instrument of aggression and assault against our spiritual enemy. The Bible says in James 4:7, "…Resist the devil, and he will flee from you."

The sword is a one-on-one weapon. It was designed for close combat. This was not a weapon of mass assault or destruction, but rather one used in personal conflict. The Word of God is the Holy Spirit's weapon in your personal, daily battle of the flesh against the Spirit.

The sword is a piercing weapon. It was designed to penetrate the enemy, to be thrust toward the enemy, and to fend off attack. It was used to place the enemy in a defensive posture or to cause the enemy to retreat. Even so, the Word of God is designed to be used decisively in spiritual battle. Hebrews 4:12 says, "For the word of God is quick, and powerful, and sharper than any twoedged sword, piercing even to the dividing asunder of soul and spirit, and of the joints and marrow, and is a discerner of the thoughts and intents of the heart."

Using the sword requires practice. It was a skill to be learned. The longer a soldier trained and practiced, the better he became at handling his sword. Winning with the sword required knowledge, skill, and practice. In like manner, we are commanded to study God's Word, to search out the Scriptures, that we might become skillful in spiritual battle. Second Timothy 2:15 says, "Study to shew thyself approved unto God, a workman that needeth not to be ashamed, rightly dividing the word of truth." And Acts 17:11 speaks of searching the Scriptures, "These were more noble than those in Thessalonica, in that they received the word with all readiness of mind, and searched the scriptures daily, whether those things were so." How well we learn to use the Sword of the Spirit will determine our success in daily spiritual battle.

THE HOLY SPIRIT USES SCRIPTURES

C.H. Spurgeon made the following statement about the Word of God: "God, by His Spirit, brings old truth home to the heart, gives new light to our eyes, and causes the Word to exercise new power over us, but He reveals no new facts, and He utters no words in any man's ears concerning his condition and state. We must be content with the old revelation and with the life and power and force with which the Holy Spirit brings it to the heart. Neither must any of us seek to have any additional revelation, for that would imply that the Scriptures are incomplete."

God tells us in 2 Timothy 3:16, "All scripture is given by inspiration of God, and is profitable for doctrine, for reproof, for correction, for instruction in righteousness." Consider how the Holy Spirit makes God's Word profitable in our lives:

> **How well we learn to use the Sword of the Spirit will determine our success in daily spiritual battle.**

First, the Word of God was inspired by the Spirit. Second Peter 1:21, "For the prophecy came not in old time by the will of man: but holy men of God spake as they were moved by the Holy Ghost." Acts 1:16, "Men and brethren, this scripture must needs have been fulfilled, which the Holy Ghost by the mouth of David spake before concerning Judas, which was guide to them that took Jesus."

Second, the Word of God is explained by the Spirit. As we saw earlier, the Holy Spirit teaches us God's Word and reveals God's heart to us. This is explained with great clarity in 1 Corinthians 2:9–13:

> *But as it is written, Eye hath not seen, nor ear heard,*
> *neither have entered into the heart of man, the things*
> *which God hath prepared for them that love him. But*

God hath revealed them unto us by his Spirit: for the Spirit searcheth all things, yea, the deep things of God. For what man knoweth the things of a man, save the spirit of man which is in him? even so the things of God knoweth no man, but the Spirit of God. Now we have received, not the spirit of the world, but the spirit which is of God; that we might know the things that are freely given to us of God. Which things also we speak, not in the words which man's wisdom teacheth, but which the Holy Ghost teacheth; comparing spiritual things with spiritual.

God's Word and God's Spirit work together to accomplish God's will—both in us and through us. Don Lyon wrote, "If you have the Spirit without the Word, you blow up. If you have the Word without the Spirit, you dry up. If you have both the Word and the Spirit, you grow up."

THE POWER OF THE SWORD

When it comes to winning the daily battle of the Christian life, every child of God has been given two exceedingly powerful resources—the Holy Spirit of God and the inspired Word of God. Daily victory is well within reach of every Christian. Yes, the Christian life is impossible to live by human strength, but God calls us to live beyond our capacity. And to make such a thing possible, He places His Spirit *within* us and His Word *before* us.

The problem is not that victory is elusive or difficult. The problem is not that we are so weak and our flesh is so strong. The problem is not that the devil is so cunning and that temptation is so forceful. The problem is that our Bibles are unread, unused, and unstudied, and the Holy Spirit is ignored and unwelcome. At our fingertips we have the explosive power of the very Word of God. And one breath away, we have the all-powerful Spirit of God. Yet, for love of sin and the flesh, we hold them both at bay, forbidding the power of God to truly work in our lives. We lose our battles not because we *cannot* win, but because we *will* not.

> Every child of God has been given two powerful resources—the Spirit of God and the Word of God.

Imagine if David had not slung the stone or if Joshua had not led the march around Jericho. Imagine if Noah had not boarded the ark or Gideon had not blown the trumpet. Imagine if Peter had not thrown out the net or if Namaan had not dipped the seventh time. Imagine if Daniel had not tested the prince of the eunuchs or if Elijah had not called on God. All throughout Scripture we see God's people, by faith, using the power He places before them, and as a result, God brings victory.

All of that same power is before you and within you. The very purpose of this book is to reveal it to you. Now what will you do with it? You could say, "But what is one book and an invisible Spirit against such strong temptations? What is prayer or reading against such powerful circumstances?" This is the breaking point—your faith. The Word of God is powerful. The Spirit of God is powerful. Whether you believe it or not, whether you claim it or not, these things are true.

Again, Hebrews 4:12 says, "For the word of God is quick, and powerful, and sharper than any twoedged sword, piercing even to the dividing asunder of soul and spirit, and of the joints and marrow, and is a discerner of the thoughts and intents of the heart."

Ezekiel 33:31–32 bears record that it's possible to hear the Word of God and yet do nothing with it. It describes people who say they love to hear God's Word and even express a favorable response to it, but they never allow the Holy Spirit to bring real heart change through it. They never really respond to it. "And they come unto thee as the people cometh, and they sit before thee as my people, and they hear thy words, but they will not do them: for with their mouth they shew much love, but their heart goeth after their covetousness. And, lo, thou art unto them as a very lovely song of one that hath a pleasant voice, and can play well on an instrument: for they hear thy words, but they do them not."

I beg you to avail yourself of the power of the Spirit and the power of God's Word. Daily victory is within your reach, but it calls for a response from you. Act in faith and begin actively engaging in battle by His Spirit and with His Sword.

LEARNING TO USE THE SWORD

D.L. Moody once said, "A Bible that is falling apart usually belongs to someone who is not." In order for the Word of God to make a difference we must practice its use. Practically speaking, I believe there are six simple ways you can learn to use the Sword of the Spirit to live in victory in your daily life:

Desire the Word. A growing Christian will have a natural and growing hunger to know more of God's truth. First Peter 2:2, "As newborn babes, desire the sincere milk of the word, that ye may grow thereby."

Study the Word. We are commanded to personally dig into God's Word and learn it. Second Timothy 2:15, "Study to shew thyself approved unto God, a workman that needeth not to be ashamed, rightly dividing the word of truth."

Memorize the Word. Daily or weekly choose a portion of Scripture to memorize. Psalm 119:11–12, "Thy word have I hid in mine heart, that I might not sin against thee. Blessed art thou, O LORD: teach me thy statutes."

Hear the Word. Get before the regular teaching and preaching of God's truth in a local church. Turn away from pop-psychology and avail yourself of solid, Bible teaching and preaching. First Thessalonians 2:13, "For this cause also thank we God without ceasing, because, when ye received the word of God which ye heard of us, ye received it not as the word of men, but as it is in truth, the word of God, which effectually worketh also in you that believe."

Meditate upon the Word. Think about God's truth and let your heart contemplate it throughout the day. Joshua 1:8, "This book of the law shall not depart out of thy mouth; but thou shalt meditate therein day and night, that thou mayest observe to do according to all that is written therein: for then thou shalt make thy way prosperous, and then thou shalt have good success."

Obey the Word. This boils down to simple obedience. Appropriate its truth and live by it. Apply it to your life and just do it. Psalm 119:105, "Thy word is a lamp unto my feet, and a light unto my path." James 1:25, "But whoso looketh into the perfect law of liberty, and continueth therein, he being not a forgetful hearer, but a doer of the work, this man shall be blessed in his deed."

One afternoon in 1986, when I was new in Lancaster, I was out knocking on doors to invite people to church. The Lord led me that day to a providential encounter with an elderly man I will never forget. His name was Harley Peters.

After I introduced myself, he invited me into his home where we sat down and began to talk. There I began one of the most cherished and helpful relationships of my entire ministry. I invited Harley to our young church, and immediately he began asking me questions. Nearly every single question related to God's Word in some way. He asked about doctrine, philosophy, and practice.

Thankfully, I passed his test, and not long after that, Harley and his wife Bernice joined Lancaster Baptist Church. Over the years the Peters became two of my greatest prayer warriors and encouragers in ministry. They were Spirit-filled Christians who knew the Word of God well.

Several years after they became members of our church, Harley's health began to deteriorate and he was unable to attend church as often as he would have liked. Even through his health trials, Harley Peters remained a tremendous source of encouragement to me. He was a godly man whose life clearly demonstrated spiritual success. He was a faithful husband for sixty-seven years.

After several years of health trials, the Lord took Harley home to Heaven. Sometime after the home-going service, his daughter gave me his Bible and asked me to keep it. To this day it is a cherished gift that resides in my office. I will never forget the first of many times I leafed through its well-worn pages. The secret of Harley's spiritual success was evident—he loved his Bible. Every single page was marked or notated in some way. Passage after passage was underlined, explained, and cross-referenced—and not by a preacher, but by an aerospace worker who loved God's Word.

Harley fell in love with God's Word, and in so doing, he availed himself of the Holy Spirit and the Sword. He lived a victorious Christian life because he let God's Spirit use God's Word to transform his life. This is the same work the Spirit of God desires to do in you.

As you allow the Holy Spirit to engrave His Word into your heart and change your life, you become a living epistle: a "walking Bible." Second Corinthians 3:2–3 says, "Ye are our epistle written in our hearts, known and read of all men: Forasmuch as ye are manifestly declared to be the epistle of Christ ministered by us, written not with ink, but with the Spirit of the living God; not in tables of stone, but in fleshy tables of the heart."

Ask the Holy Spirit of God to stir within you a fresh and enduring love for God's Word—the Sword of the Spirit. Decide right now that a day will not go by when you don't avail yourself of the mighty power of this Sword. For in so doing, you will discover that no sin, no temptation, and no fleshly desire is a match for the power of God's Spirit using God's Word in your life.

EIGHT

THE STREAM OF
THE SPIRIT (PART ONE)

O ne of my favorite places is my grandfather's farm in southwestern Colorado, near Cortez. I have a thousand cherished childhood adventures flowing from that old farmhouse and those rows of beans. From shooting guns off the canyon rim to laboring in the fields to eating fresh raspberries and ice cream, my heart returns to childhood every time I visit this wonderful place.

As my children were growing up, the farm was also one of our favorite vacation destinations. The drive across Arizona was always long, but the anticipation of arriving and soon thereafter biting into fresh fruit from the orchard was always enough to keep the whole family going. It never failed, as soon as we pulled into the dirt driveway, Grandad would meet us at the car. Before we could even unload our luggage or hug the rest of the family, he would say, "Let's go check the garden."

On a recent trip, things were radically different. The orchard, usually abundant with fruit, was bare. The bountiful fruit trees were gone, and all that remained were two sickly looking trees with no signs of fruit. When I asked my uncle what happened, he told me that a recent drought had killed the trees. Without the necessary water and nutrients to sustain life, the expected fruit did not appear.

Such is the Christian life—we are organic. It all starts in the fertile soil of a soft heart, seeded with the Word of God, and then nourished with the watering presence of the Holy Spirit. Our spiritual lives are made to grow from these three elements working together. Exposure to the right spiritual nutrients and elements triggers a natural process of transformation and fruit bearing.

To the contrary, like those trees, it is possible to become discouraged, distracted, and disinterested until we stop growing. When properly nourished by God's Spirit, our lives remain full and fruitful. But when the spiritual life is neglected we dry up and wither in fruitlessness. Wouldn't you prefer to remain full and fruitful?

Thus far in part two of this book, we've seen the struggle of the flesh against the Spirit, and we've seen the Sword (or seed) of the Word of God. Now we will discover the wonderful results of letting the Holy Spirit do His work within. It's called *fruit*, and the Bible has a lot to say about being a fruitful Christian.

ABIDING IN THE VINE

John 15:1–4 says, "I am the true vine, and my Father is the husbandman. Every branch in me that beareth not fruit he taketh away: and every branch that beareth fruit, he purgeth it, that it may bring forth more fruit. Now ye are clean through the word which I have spoken unto you. Abide in me, and I in you. As the branch cannot bear fruit of itself, except it abide in the vine; no more can ye, except ye abide in me."

All fruitfulness begins with Jesus. This passage teaches us that He is the source—the Vine—and we are but branches, receiving our nutrients and life from Him. And the point of this passage is that the Lord wants us to continually bear fruit that glorifies Him.

There is nothing good about you or me, except Jesus Christ and the Holy Spirit at work in our lives. Apart from Him we can do nothing. In our own selves, fruit does not grow naturally; weeds grow naturally. But when we maintain a daily, dependent, abiding relationship with Christ our lives take on the supernatural growth cycle that we've been studying throughout this book.

One purpose of this abiding relationship is that fruit might abound outwardly—that our lives might make manifest the presence of God. The Bible says in Matthew 7:20, "Wherefore by their fruits ye shall know them." Fruit is the outward sign of the presence and power of God. It is what will convince a lost world that your relationship with God is genuine, and will cause others to see God's unquestionable power in your life.

Consider this for a moment: when others spend time with you or see your life, do they see unquestionable evidence of God? Is there anything remarkable or outstanding growing in your life? Are you exhibiting any qualities that would indicate a supernatural, transformational work taking place inside of you?

There is nothing more attractive to a lost world than a Christian radiating the fruit of the Holy Spirit.

Christians who live in the power of the Holy Spirit are a marvel to the secular world. Their joy, their sincerity, their humility, and their peace are both ridiculed and envied at the same time. The qualities we are about to study are what make Christianity attractive to the lost. They are outstanding. They are virtuous. They are excellent in every way.

Most importantly, this fruit is the natural product of a nourishing relationship with the Holy Spirit of God. It is not produced by self-will or iron determination. It is produced by God's Spirit. You choose to abide in the Vine, and fruit will flow forth naturally.

There is nothing more attractive and compelling to a lost world than a Christian radiating the fruit of the Holy Spirit. Let's take a brief look at what the Spirit of God desires to create in you.

THE FRUIT OF THE SPIRIT

> *But the fruit of the Spirit is love, joy, peace, longsuffering, gentleness, goodness, faith, Meekness, temperance: against such there is no law.*
> —GALATIANS 5:22–23

It is important to note that God uses the singular form of fruit. These are not "fruits," they are fruit. They come together as a singular result of the work of the Holy Spirit in our lives.

THE HOLY SPIRIT PRODUCES LOVE

Have you ever read the newspaper or watched the news and found yourself asking, "Whatever happened to love? Whatever happened to people who truly care about another's needs?" The Bible says that love is the first fruit of the Spirit. In our culture, people are starving for love, and they are looking for it in all the wrong places.

A popular song from years ago called love "nothing but a second-hand emotion." This is about as good as it gets in the world's eyes. No matter how hard the world searches, true love eludes someone who does not know God. According to Him, the only way to experience true love and to show true love is through the Holy Spirit.

First Corinthians 13 is the Bible's most well-known passage about love. It summarizes love in the following ways: Love is patient. Love is kind. Love is not jealous. Love does not brag. Love is not arrogant. Love does not behave unbecomingly. Love does not seek its own. Love is not easily provoked. Love does not harbor evil.

Look at that list again. You could work ten lifetimes and never perfect that list. Or you could yield to the Holy Spirit each day, and let this fruit grow.

THE HOLY SPIRIT PRODUCES JOY

Since the beginning of time, men have sought for true and lasting joy in things that only bring temporal happiness. Look at what some of the most well-known figures of history had to say about their life journey:

The infidel Voltaire wrote, "I wish I had never been born."

Lord Byron, who lived a life of pleasure, said, "The worm, the canker, and grief are mine alone."

Jay Gould, the American millionaire, stated, "I suppose I am the most miserable man on earth."

Lord Beaconsfield quoted, "Youth is a mistake; manhood a struggle; old age a regret."

Alexander the Great, after conquering the known world, wept, "There are no more worlds to conquer."

Jim Loeher in *The Power of Full Engagement* gave an interesting statistic: "Researchers have found no correlation between income levels and happiness. Between 1957 and 1990, income levels in the U.S. doubled. Yet at the same period, people's levels of happiness did not increase. In fact, reports of depression actually increased ten fold. Incidents of divorce, suicide, alcoholism, and drug abuse also rose dramatically."

In search of joy, most men grasp for money, possessions, fame, power, or painkillers. But all of these leave the heart destitute and disappointed. The Holy Spirit's fruit of joy, however, runs so deep, you can even experience it through suffering. God says, "Even when you are suffering, I can give you joy." First Peter 1:6 says, "Wherein ye greatly rejoice, though now for a season, if need be, ye are in heaviness through manifold temptations."

The book of 1 Peter was written to Christians who were facing extreme persecution for their faith. Read carefully how joy rises above their deep trials: "That the trial of your faith, being much more precious than of gold that perisheth, though it be tried with fire, might be found unto praise and honour and glory at the appearing of Jesus Christ: Whom having not seen, ye love; in whom, though now ye see him not, yet believing, ye rejoice with joy unspeakable and full of glory" (1 Peter 1:7–8). Joy unspeakable! It's an indescribable kind of happiness.

THE HOLY SPIRIT PRODUCES PEACE

According to recent studies, the world has known only 292 years of peace since 3,600 BC. Since that year, there have been 14,351 wars in which 3.64 billion people have died. In addition, it is remarkable that over 8,000 peace treaties have been made and broken over the same period of time.

The world longs for peace—world peace, peace of mind, and inner peace. We hear about it from the media every day. People are turning to yoga, transcendental meditation, and every form of religion.

Many years ago a man searched for the perfect picture of peace. Not finding any that satisfied him, he announced a painting contest centered on this theme. Artists' imaginations were stirred by this challenge, and paintings from around the world soon began to arrive. It was finally the day of revelation. Judges uncovered one peaceful scene after another while viewers clapped and cheered.

Tension grew. Only two veiled pictures remained. As the judge pulled the cover from one, a hush fell over the crowd. A mirror-smooth lake reflected lacy, green birches under the soft blush of the evening sky. Along the grassy shore, a flock of sheep was grazing undisturbed. Surely this painting was the winner.

As the final painting was uncovered, the crowd gasped in surprise. Could this be peace? Surely the artist misunderstood the contest. A tumultuous waterfall cascaded down a rocky precipice. The crowd could almost feel its cold, penetrating spray. Above it, stormy-gray clouds threatened to explode with lightning, wind, and rain. In the midst of the thundering billows and bitter chill, a spindly tree clung to the rocks at the edge of the falls. One of its branches reached out in front of the torrential waters as if foolishly seeking to experience its full power. In the elbow of that branch, a little bird had built a nest. Content and undisturbed, ready to cover her little ones in her wings, she manifested peace that transcends all earthly turmoil.

Peace is not being where there is no storm or difficulty. Peace is being in the midst of all those things and remaining calm in your heart.

> Peace is not being where there is no storm or difficulty. Peace is being in the midst of all those things and remaining calm in your heart.

Philippians 4:6–7 says, "Be careful for nothing; but in every thing by prayer and supplication with thanksgiving let your requests be made known unto God. And the peace of God, which passeth all understanding, shall keep your hearts and minds through Christ Jesus." The word *worry* is from the German word *wergen* which means to choke. When we are worried and stressed, it chokes out our ability to concentrate, to serve, and to make right decisions.

When I was living in Korea as a teenager, I heard about some Korean Christians who were being persecuted for their faith. In response to their persecution they said, "We are like nails. The harder you drive us, the deeper you drive us. The deeper you drive us, the more peaceful it becomes."

These examples provide us with the right picture of the fruit of peace. When the Holy Spirit produces peace, it doesn't matter how great the pressure is in your life—it only matters that the pressure pushes you closer to Jesus Christ. Isaiah 26:3 says, "Thou wilt keep him in perfect peace, whose mind is stayed on thee: because he trusteth in thee." And Colossians 3:15 encourages us to "let the peace of God rule in your hearts."

The peace we find in the Holy Spirit is a peace that rules over the soul. What a beautiful thought. When your soul is burdened down with agitations, overwhelmed with excitement, or tired from worry, the peace of God will preside over you with a sense of calmness. Someone once said, "Sometimes the Lord rides out the storm with us and other times He calms the restless sea around us. Most of all, He calms the storm inside us in our deepest inner soul."

THE HOLY SPIRIT PRODUCES LONGSUFFERING

Many people who live in Indio, California, are proud of a particular fruit that grows in their specific desert environment and climate— dates. Date palm trees live a very long time. They are unique in that they don't begin to bear fruit until their fourth year, and their fruit bearing does not become prosperous until approximately their eightieth year. By that time, a date palm tree produces approximately one hundred pounds of fruit on an annual basis. The trees don't reach their full potential until they are one hundred years old.

The date palm is a beautiful picture of longsuffering. The English word longsuffering comes from two Greek words which mean slow to wrath. This is a Holy Spirit developed quality of endurance that patiently waits without becoming angry.

We live in a day of quick fixes. From text messages and e-mail to FedEx and fast food, we are accustomed to immediate gratification. Let's face it, in the twenty-first century, we don't like to wait on anything—especially things or people that frustrate us.

I read that when Abraham Lincoln practiced law, he was approached by a man who desperately wanted revenge against a fellow who owed him money. He begged Lincoln to bring a lawsuit for a mere $2.50 against this debtor. Seeing through the man's unreasonable obsession, Lincoln did all he could to discourage him of such a lawsuit, but to no avail—the man insisted on bringing legal action.

At last, unable to persuade him otherwise, Lincoln agreed to take the case, but only if he could pay the legal fee of $10 upfront. The plaintiff eagerly paid the money. Then, in an unexpected turn of events, Lincoln immediately gave half of the legal fees to the defendant who confessed to the debt and paid it off. Vengeance cost the man a lot more than longsuffering would have!

Someone once said, "Longsuffering is the grace of a man who could revenge himself but does not."

In my Christian life, there have been overwhelming times of anguish when I could do nothing but wait and endure. In those times, I believe the Holy Spirit gave me the fruit of longsuffering. I have not always understood the purpose of trials and hardship, but I have always known the work of the Holy Spirit during such times.

Are you exhibiting the fruit of love, joy, peace, and longsuffering? Before salvation, these qualities would not have naturally flowed from within you. Thankfully, the stream of the Holy Spirit can begin today what will eventually be an abundant harvest.

Before moving on to the last five in this list of fruit, take a moment to thank the Lord for His presence in your life, and yield to the stream of the Holy Spirit that His fruit might become more evident in you.

NINE

THE STREAM OF
THE SPIRIT (PART TWO)

I recently heard about two brothers who were playing in their room. The two-year-old reached up and yanked his older brother's hair. His mother heard him scream in pain, and rushed in to take care of the situation. After hearing what had happened, she told her older son, "Well, your brother is only two years old, and he doesn't know what it's like to have his hair pulled."

Moments later, the mother heard another scream, this time coming from the two-year-old. She rushed into the room and asked what was wrong. Her older son replied, "Now he knows!"

Our natural responses are usually wrong. Why? Because in our flesh resides the power of sin. Left to our own, we do not naturally produce the fruit of love, joy, peace, longsuffering, gentleness, goodness, meekness, faith, or temperance.

Let's briefly look at the last five in the list of the fruit of the Holy Spirit:

THE HOLY SPIRIT PRODUCES GENTLENESS

What do you think of when you hear the word gentleness? Does the term *dentist* come to mind? For some reason I don't immediately equate dentist with gentleness, rather I think of expressions like *pain* or *infliction*, even though my dentist does a good job of inflicting pain gently. When I think of gentleness, I think of mothers. They have a way of being sympathetic and encouraging when things are rough. They have a way of expressing compassion and comfort.

Webster defines gentleness as "being generous and kind." Benjamin Franklin often tried to encourage his children to be gentle with this thought, "I will speak ill of no man, not even in the matter of truth, but rather excuse the faults I hear, and, upon proper occasions, speak all the good I know of everybody." That was Benjamin Franklin's desire—to be a gentle man.

If I interviewed your family and friends, could they describe you as *gentle*? As you yield to the Holy Spirit, you will become a more gentle person by nature.

The Apostle Paul illustrated this kind of gentleness as he ministered to the new Christians in 1 Thessalonians 2:7, "But we were gentle among you, even as a nurse cherisheth her children."

Paul was a strong Gospel preacher, yet he realized the importance of being a compassionate servant.

Many people have a distorted view of God—limited only to His wrath. Yes, God hates sin, but He loves people. He is the ultimate expression of love, longsuffering, and gentleness. He is the perfect Father, and He desires for His perfect qualities to flow from your life.

I want to challenge you to seek to display God's gentleness in all of your relationships in four key ways: sensitivity, sympathy, straightforwardness, and spontaneity.

Sensitivity sees and experiences life from the emotions and feelings of others. It considers others and seeks to patiently identify with and understand what they are going through.

Sympathy feels what others feel, and acknowledges those feelings. It bears the burden and feels the hurt. It rejoices with those that rejoice and weeps with those that weep.

Straightforwardness speaks the truth in love. It doesn't avoid uncomfortable conversations. But it seeks to deliver them with kindness and care.

Spontaneity is thoughtfulness in action. It seeks to express gentleness in small, accessible ways. It's always looking for some way to serve or give care.

You will either be gentle or grumpy. It's your call. In your natural state, grumpy will usually be the order of the day—especially when things don't go your way. By His Spirit, gentleness will be one of your most attractive qualities.

THE HOLY SPIRIT PRODUCES GOODNESS

In every relationship there are toxins or potential elements with destructive capacity. Yet God, through the Holy Spirit, has provided a cleansing agent for restored vitality in your relationships. This agent is the attribute of goodness.

> *For ye were sometimes darkness, but now are ye light*
> *in the Lord: walk as children of light: (For the fruit*
> *of the Spirit is in all goodness and righteousness and*
> *truth;) Proving what is acceptable unto the Lord.*
> —EPHESIANS 5:8–10

The spiritual fruit of goodness is defined as "uprightness of heart and life; virtue equipped and ready at every point." Galatians 6:10 says, "As we have therefore opportunity, let us do good unto all men, especially unto them who are of the household of faith." A Spirit-filled Christian naturally desires to do good for others. Being good is what you are on the inside, doing good is what people see on the outside.

In the early church, Christians often faced criticism and slander. Instead of complaining or quitting, they handled their critics by staying faithful in good works. "Having your conversation honest among the Gentiles: that, whereas they speak against you as evildoers, they may by your good works, which they shall behold, glorify God in the day of visitation" (1 Peter 2:12).

Ten years from now, when you are still doing good, others will know you by your fruit.

THE HOLY SPIRIT PRODUCES FAITH

On July 29, 1981, one of the most highly publicized and glamorous weddings in history was celebrated. Britain's Prince Charles wed Lady Diana. This wedding was a modern fairy tale: a royal prince marries a lovely commoner in front of thousands of adoring subjects. They were the envy of the world—rich, young, and beautiful. People said theirs was a marriage made in Heaven.

Sadly, their happiness was short-lived. The fairy tale became a nightmare of infidelity and unfaithfulness.

There is a short supply of faith and faithfulness in our world today. In many circumstances, we give up too soon. Commitment is rare and perseverance almost nonexistent. By nature we choose the path of least resistance. We choose the path that promises immediate gratification. But in God's strength, the right path is always the one that grows in faith and persists in faithfulness. It's the path of no retreat, and it's always the path of greatest reward.

Since 1986, the Holy Spirit of God has been doing a great work of faith and faithfulness in my life and in the lives of the church family at Lancaster Baptist Church. As a part of that work, He has continually led us into building programs and campus development projects, to make space for the many He would touch through this ministry. At countless points along the way it seemed easier for all of us to stop pressing forward in faith. The spiritual opposition was great. The obstacles seemed insurmountable. But the Spirit compelled us to continue expressing faith and living faithfully. Today our campus is still being developed, but by God's grace and to His glory, a fifty-million dollar campus exists because God's people were willing to continue in faith.

When yielding to the Holy Spirit, you will grow in faith, and as a result, you will persist with faithfulness in all of the right areas of life. The result will be well worth the perseverance.

> Your faithfulness is of much more value to God than your talents, abilities, or skills.

Yellowstone is one of our nation's most beautiful and famous national parks. One of its most popular features is a geyser named Old Faithful. This geyser was named because of its predictability and punctuality, and people travel from all over the world to see Old Faithful in action. What has made Old Faithful a tourism hot spot? Is it the breathtaking beauty or spectacular performance? No, this geyser is known and praised for its dependability.

Similarly, your faithfulness as a Christian is of much more value to God than your talents, abilities, or skills. And through His Spirit, He offers to make you a person of faith and faithfulness.

THE HOLY SPIRIT PRODUCES MEEKNESS

In Matthew 5:5 Jesus said, "Blessed are the meek: for they shall inherit the earth." Again in Matthew 11:29 He said, "Take my yoke upon you, and learn of me; for I am meek and lowly in heart: and ye shall find rest unto your souls."

In His Word, God often refers to us as sheep. Honestly, sheep are among the dumbest, neediest, most dependent animals in the world. You've probably never heard of a sports team named the "Mighty, Mighty... Sheep."

Secular culture has a significantly different view of self. The natural man is not discovering how to be more meek. He's bent on being more assertive. The voices of secular media remind us of self-promotion, self-gratification, and self-obsession. We live in a very narcissistic day. Against the landscape of magazines like *Self*, *Glamour*, and *Vanity Fair*, we're not seeing a lot of publishers fighting for the name *Meekness*! The natural man is opposed to the virtues of humility and meekness. Life is all about *my rights* or *my image* and looking out for "number one."

Yet, when the Holy Spirit's stream is flowing, He will always grow the fruit of meekness. Meekness is defined as a submissive or teachable spirit toward God that reveals itself in genuine consideration to others. It is directed first toward God and then toward fellow man.

Consider the admonitions of Scripture to believers concerning meekness:

*In meekness instructing those that oppose themselves;
if God peradventure will give them repentance to the
acknowledging of the truth.*—2 TIMOTHY 2:25

*To speak evil of no man, to be no brawlers, but gentle,
shewing all meekness unto all men.*—TITUS 3:2

*Wherefore lay apart all filthiness and superfluity of
naughtiness, and receive with meekness the engrafted
word, which is able to save your souls.*—JAMES 1:21

*Who is a wise man and endued with knowledge
among you? let him shew out of a good conversation
his works with meekness of wisdom.*—JAMES 3:13

Many people fail to understand that meekness is not weakness. Meekness is actually strength under control—power under the influence of restraint. Consider Jesus. He is the perfect example of meekness, and yet He has all power. In His almightiness, He humbled Himself. With all of the power in the universe, He chose to put it under control so that He might become your Saviour. The death of Christ on the Cross painted a portrait of what ultimate power under control looks like—meekness.

The display of meekness requires uncommon strength—the sort of strength you can only find in the Holy Spirit. Think about it. Your flesh desires to fly off the handle and speak your mind. Your flesh will compel you to fight for yourself in every situation. But the Holy Spirit of God will produce a different set of responses. Meekness is the strength to back away from a fight you could win. It is the ability to handle hurt without overreacting.

A missionary in Jamaica was once questioning some little boys on the meaning of Matthew 5:5. He asked, "Who are the meek?" One child answered, "Those who give soft answers to rough questions."

THE HOLY SPIRIT PRODUCES TEMPERANCE

Years ago, Stanford University conducted a study on preschoolers. The children were each given a marshmallow and two options: they could have one marshmallow immediately, or they could have two marshmallows later—after the experimenter returned from an errand. As the adult left the room and left the decision up to the kids, it was interesting to see the responses.

> Meekness is the strength to back away from a fight you could win.

Some of the youngsters gave up waiting and devoured the treat right away. Others waited for what seemed like an eternity, hoping to cash in on two. The waiting children became fidgety and did whatever they could to refrain from eating their marshmallows. They covered their eyes, talked to themselves, sang, and attempted to sleep. A short twenty minutes later they were rewarded with a second marshmallow.

During a follow-up study years later, the researchers uncovered some interesting information. The children who had been able to wait for the two marshmallows became adolescents with a greater ability to endure delayed gratification in pursuing their life's goals. In contrast, the kids who grabbed the one marshmallow were, as adolescents, more likely to be stubborn, indecisive, and stressed. The study revealed the power of self-restraint and the frustration of a life without it.

Many problems in life are related to a lack of temperance. The dictionary defines temperance as "self-control or discretion." A temperate person knows what is best and has the self-control to act upon that knowledge.

> Spiritual people are not known for lies, gossip, slander, insult, or verbal injury.

Another definition of temperance is "discipline." Paul said in 1 Corinthians 9:24–27, "Know ye not that they which run in a race run all, but one receiveth the prize? So run, that ye may obtain. And every man that striveth for the mastery is temperate in all things. Now they do it to obtain a corruptible crown; but we an incorruptible. I therefore so run, not as uncertainly; so fight I, not as one that beateth the air: But I keep under my body, and bring it into subjection: lest that by any means, when I have preached to others, I myself should be a castaway."

In this passage, Paul compared the Christian life to an athlete running a race—to the Olympian whose life is characterized by discipline and self-control. Likewise, our high calling in Christ demands a disciplined life.

When you yield to the Holy Spirit's power, temperance will show up in three primary areas:

A Disciplined Physical Life. A person filled with the Holy Spirit has the power of God to say "no" to things that are not best for his mental and physical well-being. Whether it's ordering your life by God's priorities, caring for your body, or expressing financial wisdom and restraint, the power of the Spirit makes a disciplined life possible.

The story is told of Sandy McIntyre who, during the days of northern Ontario's gold rush, found the now famous mine bearing his name. Just days after discovering the mine, McIntyre sold his deed for twenty-five dollars to buy a glass of liquor. A vein was found shortly thereafter that produced over 230 million dollars worth of gold.

Throughout history, whether because of alcohol, lust, or hatred, men and women have acted in indescribable and unthinkable ways because of a lack of the fruit of temperance.

A Disciplined Speech. Those bearing the fruit of temperance will know what to say and what to refrain from saying. God's Word says, "Let no corrupt communication proceed out of your mouth, but that which is good to the use of edifying, that it may minister grace unto the hearers" (Ephesians 4:29).

Spiritual people are not known for lies, gossip, slander, insult, or verbal injury. They don't go running off at the mouth. They intentionally use their speech for that which is good—encouraging and edifying others.

A Disciplined Mind. Temperance is also manifested by controlled thoughts. Second Corinthians 10:5 states, "Casting down imaginations, and every high thing that exalteth itself against the knowledge of God, and bringing into captivity every thought to the obedience of Christ." The word *imaginations* means thoughts or fantasies against the truth of Christ or the revealed will of God. The mind and thoughts of a Spirit-controlled man will be distinctly different from the mind of a carnal man.

A man once bought a quaint home with a small yet sturdy tree in the backyard. It was winter, and nothing marked this tree as different from any other tree. When spring came, the tree began to grow leaves and tiny pink buds. "How wonderful," thought the man, "I own a tree with exquisite pink flowers. I am going to enjoy its beauty all summer!" Before he had time to enjoy the beauty of the tree, the wind began to blow and soon all the petals were strewn in the yard.

"What a mess," he thought. "This tree isn't any use after all."

The summer passed, and one day the man noticed the tree was producing green fruit the size of large nuts. He cautiously picked one and took a bite. "Yuck!" he exclaimed, throwing it to the ground. "What an awful taste! This tree is worthless. Its flowers are so delicate the wind blows them away, and its fruit is extremely bitter. When winter comes, I'm definitely cutting down this tree."

The tree took no notice of the man and continued to draw warmth from the sun and water from the ground. When late fall came, the tree began to produce crisp, red apples.

The tree did not bear fruit in the beginning stages of its existence, because it first had to endure a period of growth. When the time was right, fruit came forth in abundance. Even so, you are meant to bear fruit, but you can only do so as you grow in the Holy Spirit and walk with Him.

The fruit of the Spirit is motivating in two ways:

First, it represents nine attractive and virtuous qualities that we all desire. This fruit is not sensational or self exalting in any way. It is the display of Christ-like character with sincerity and humility. It compels us to abide in Christ that the fruit might come forth. Second, this fruit is evidence of a right relationship with God. The absence of fruit is convicting because it reveals the lack of a faithful, private walk with Christ.

Likewise, the fruit of the Spirit can be frustrating in two ways. First, bearing fruit takes time and growth. It's easy to become impatient and wish the process were faster. Second, the fruit cannot be manufactured artificially. Genuine fruit requires a genuine walk in the Spirit. Trying to produce this fruit apart from the Holy Spirit is frustrating because it's impossible.

Have you ever heard the phrase "like father, like son"? Children often bear a close resemblance to their parents and grandparents—even in the most subtle of ways. It's entertaining and amazing to see a young child subconsciously pick up on subtleties of their parents—small gestures, vocal inflections, facial expressions, and physical attributes. In fact, with a little time spent in a mixed group of families, a discerning mind wouldn't have much trouble putting kids and parents together. Similar traits show up easily.

Even so, in the Christian life, the Holy Spirit would like to transform you into the image of Christ. He would like you to bear a striking resemblance to your Heavenly Father.

Wouldn't it be awesome if people who knew you were able to quickly discern qualities in your life that reminded them of the character of Christ? Wouldn't it be great to hear, "Hey, you're a lot like your Father!"

Since the Holy Spirit lives in you, His fruit makes it all possible.

TEN

THE SUPPLY OF THE SPIRIT

I recently read about a lady who was late in sending her Christmas cards out. Time got away from her, and in a rush, she hurriedly bought, signed, and sent forty-nine Christmas cards. In the hurry, she failed to take time to read the message on the inside.

On Christmas Day, she noticed the one remaining card she hadn't sent and took a minute to read it: "Just a little note to say… A special gift is on its way." Suddenly she realized with horror that forty-nine of her friends were now expecting a gift from her!

Everybody likes to receive gifts, and in this chapter we're going to discover that the Holy Spirit provides every child of God with one or more gifts—spiritual gifts. God teaches us in His Word about the gifts of the Spirit. These gifts tie into the divine enabling that we studied earlier. They are special abilities given to us at salvation for the express purpose of serving God and fulfilling His call. Your gift perfectly matches your calling. It's what you love to do. It's what you're naturally good at—by His Spirit. It's what you can do best to serve God and His people.

Few Christians ever understand spiritual gifts, much less discover their own gifts and use them for God's work. But one of the most important things you can do after salvation is to discover, develop, and deploy your spiritual gifts in the service of God. Nothing will ignite your passion for ministry and your joy in the Lord more than using your divine enabling for His glory. Serving in the area of your giftedness is beyond enjoyable. It's one of the most rewarding and fulfilling experiences in the Christian life.

> Your spiritual gift is what you can do best to serve God and His people.

If the mention of spiritual gifts brings up images of "charismatic sensationalism" like talking in tongues, healing, drinking poison, and other strange phenomenon, please know that those gifts passed off the scene of Christendom in the first century. They were temporary, miraculous abilities that the disciples were given in the apostolic age to prove and validate their message. They are often called "sign gifts" because they were given temporarily for a sign to the Jews who would not believe. The temporary sign gifts were used amazingly in the beginning of the church. The permanent edifying gifts are used continually in the building of the church.

The Bible indicates that the sign gifts would pass away and cease. Indeed they did, as the apostles died and the Scriptures were completed (1 Corinthians 13:10). (For more information about sign gifts and why they are not in use today, visit the sermon archive at lancasterbaptist.org.)

The gifts we're going to study are practical, ministry-oriented, serving gifts that were given for the edification of others. Let's take a closer look at these divinely given abilities, and then discuss discovering, developing, and deploying yours.

AN EXPLANATION OF SPIRITUAL GIFTS

When you accepted Christ, God gave you an ability by the Holy Spirit to serve Him in a unique way. He enabled you to meet a specific need in the body of your local church family. The Bible says this in 1 Peter 4:10, "As every man hath received the gift, even so minister the same one to another, as good stewards of the manifold grace of God."

Even if you don't know what it is or don't feel particularly gifted in a specific area, the Bible teaches that you do have a special gift that you can use to serve God. Think about what God says:

> *But now hath God set the members every one of them*
> *in the body, as it hath pleased him. And if they were*

all one member, where were the body? But now are they many members, yet but one body. And the eye cannot say unto the hand, I have no need of thee: nor again the head to the feet, I have no need of you. Nay, much more those members of the body, which seem to be more feeble, are necessary: And those members of the body, which we think to be less honourable, upon these we bestow more abundant honour; and our uncomely parts have more abundant comeliness. For our comely parts have no need: but God hath tempered the body together, having given more abundant honour to that part which lacked.
—1 Corinthians 12:18–24

God's Word teaches in this passage that He wants to place you into a local church family as a member that you might be a part of the body, participating in His work with your church. He teaches that you are vital to the health and strength of the rest of the body.

What should you do with your spiritual gift? Notice how Paul instructed Timothy in 2 Timothy 1:6, "Wherefore I put thee in remembrance that thou stir up the gift of God, which is in thee by the putting on of my hands." First Peter says that God wants you to be a "good steward" of His gift to you, "As every man hath received the gift, even so minister the same one to another, as good stewards of the manifold grace of God" (1 Peter 4:10).

The great result of using your gift is that others are helped. As the entire church family ministers to each other and to the community, the Gospel changes lives. That's the way the local church is supposed to work.

Too often we make church a spectator event. We attend services, listen to songs, hear sermons, and then go home. These things are vital, but local church life should be a fully engaged life—it should be an immersive experience—plunging your whole heart into participation, growth, fellowship, and service with God's people.

In Acts 2:42, the early Christians continued steadfastly. They made their spiritual growth and ministry a steadfast priority in life. This wasn't something that took a backseat in any area of life. Spiritual growth, spiritual service, and spiritual fellowship were primary. The verse says, "And they continued steadfastly in the apostles' doctrine and fellowship, and in breaking of bread, and in prayers."

These Christians grew by being fully engaged in local church life and service. The same is true for you. As you discover your God-given gift and become active in serving with it, your spiritual growth will accelerate rapidly.

WHAT ARE THE SPIRITUAL GIFTS?

Present-day spiritual gifts are summarized in God's Word—"Having then gifts differing according to the grace that is given to us, whether prophecy, let us prophesy according to the proportion of faith; Or ministry, let us wait on our ministering: or he that teacheth, on teaching; Or he that exhorteth, on exhortation: he that giveth, let him do it with simplicity; he that ruleth, with diligence; he that sheweth mercy, with cheerfulness" (Romans 12:6–8).

The spiritual gifts listed in these verses are as follows:

Prophecy. This is a gift or call from God to preach His Word. Obviously, pastors and evangelists should have this calling and gift. These Christians are passionate to declare the Word of God.

Ministry (Helps). This is a desire to serve and help God's people in a variety of ways. This gift manifests itself through a passion to serve behind the scenes. These Christians love serving and helping to make a vision reality.

Teaching. This is the ability and desire to teach God's truth and help people understand how His Word applies to their lives. These Christians love to dig into God's Word and make it understandable to the hearers.

Exhortation (Encouragement). This is the ability and desire to encourage others in the Christian life. These Christians love to lift up others with positive words and deeds.

Giving. This is the ability and desire to give to God's work and God's people. It is accompanied by the provision to give. These Christians are generous by nature and love to give to God's work.

Ruling (Administration). This is the ability to lead and administrate part of God's work. It reveals itself through natural abilities to organize, think strategically, implement a plan, or coordinate teams of people. These Christians love to bring things to order and make things happen in God's work.

Mercy. This is the God-given ability to feel the pain of others and help them during trials. Those with the gift of mercy are naturally good at sympathizing and empathizing with those carrying heavy burdens. They know what to say and have a "good bedside manner." These Christians love to visit hospitals and minister to those who are suffering.

I want to close this chapter with a simple three-part challenge for you regarding your spiritual gifts:

Discover Your Spiritual Gifts. At strivingtogether.com you will find a downloadable Spiritual Gifts Test. It won't take you long to fill out, and it's not something you can fail, so be sure to work through it. It will help you identify the areas where God has gifted you for His service.

Develop Your Spiritual Gifts. It's not uncommon to be greatly intimidated by the thought of serving God, especially if your gift puts you in front of people, teaching or leading in some way. Don't despise your gift. Embrace it—even if it leads you out of your comfort zone. Remember, this gift represents God's enabling. He intends for you to use the gifts He has given to you.

> Don't despise your gift. Embrace it—even if it leads you out of your comfort zone.

Do everything you can do to develop your gift. Use it and refine it. Read, study, and practice. The raw abilities that God has given you will mature and multiply with time and use.

Deploy Your Spiritual Gifts. Get involved. Find a local Bible-believing church where God can plug you in. Get behind the pastor, join arms with your church family, and start using your gifts to glorify Christ and bless the local church body. You are God's gift to your church, and someone in the body needs your influence. The blessing of using your gifts for others is indescribable! You're going to love using your spiritual gift in local church ministry.

I have seen some of the greatest examples of spiritual gifts in action occur on the campus of Lancaster Baptist Church and West Coast Baptist College every day of the week, and especially on Sundays. Our church family has caught the vision of using their spiritual gifts together.

Each year, those in the church family who do not know their spiritual gift are encouraged to take the test. From there, our staff helps to plug them into a ministry that fits their gifts. Occasionally, a change needs to be made because someone enlisted in a ministry for which they are not gifted. Watching a church family of differing gifts serve together with one mind is a remarkable experience—and it is life-changing for the recipients of that ministry.

From Sunday classes, to school and college classrooms, to Wednesday night Bible studies and discipleship, to all the weekly activities, those with the gifts of teaching are effectively communicating God's truth to soft hearts. Those with the gifts of helps are serving food, preparing rooms, and manicuring grounds. Those with the gift of prophecy are preaching God's Word in chapels, church services, nursing homes, and extension ministries. Those with the gift of mercy are visiting hospitals and homes, ministering to the sick and suffering. Those with the gift of encouragement are strengthening the weary, ministering to the homeless, and uplifting the discouraged. Those with the gift of giving are significantly investing into the work of God with all of their resources. Those with the gift of administration are bringing order to teams and projects—helping to bring strategy and order to vision and making it a reality.

Nobody is resenting the gifts of others. The hand isn't wishing it were a foot, and the arms aren't trying to be the head. The body is serving together in Spirit-led harmony and unity. There's nothing like a healthy local church anywhere on earth! This type of church family is extremely enjoyable to be a part of and extremely attractive to a world looking for love.

Spiritual gifts are the Holy Spirit's supply in your life—His way of equipping you to do what He has called you to do in your church. Discover your gifts. Develop them. Deploy them. Immerse yourself, by His Spirit, into a life of service for the Lord. Whatever you do, be sure to heed the admonition of 1 Timothy 4:14, "Neglect not the gift that is in thee...."

ELEVEN

THE SINS AGAINST THE SPIRIT

There once lived a man who owned a beautiful house. One day he invited a friend to live with him. The living conditions were out of this world. He provided a spacious guest room, a comfortable bed on which to sleep, and a place at his luxurious dining table. The friend gladly accepted and moved in.

As time went on, the owner of this beautiful house met another friend who fascinated him. The owner kindly invited this second friend to move into his home as well. In order to make room, the first friend, already taking up residence, had to share the spacious guest room. After a little while, he was asked to give up his comfortable bed for the stranger, and lastly, to surrender his place at the table. This change grieved the first guest enough that he eventually departed from the beautiful house.

Such is the life of many Christians. How easy it is to crowd the blessed Guest of the Holy Spirit away from His deserving place of prominence. It's easy to prevent Him from being all that God has promised. How sad that we would treat the Holy Spirit of God as an unwelcome intruder rather than the sovereign Lord.

As we turn the final corner and head down the last stretch in our journey, it is important that you understand how easy it is to offend the Spirit of God and to prevent His work in your life. The Bible teaches that there are three specific ways a Christian can sin against God's Holy Spirit and limit Him. Perhaps some of these could be viewed as connected or related in ways, but because the Scripture separates them, we will study them individually:

WE CAN LIE TO THE SPIRIT

In Acts 5:1–11, we read an account of early believers who were giving to the work of God. The Holy Spirit was moving in a mighty way and leading believers to sacrifice and labor together for the Gospel. A man named Ananias and his wife, Sapphira, were appearing to participate in the offering. They had sold a piece of property, but decided in secret to lie to the Holy Spirit. Here's the story:

> *But a certain man named Ananias, with Sapphira his wife, sold a possession, And kept back part of the price, his wife also being privy to it, and brought a certain*

part, and laid it at the apostles' feet. But Peter said, Ananias, why hath Satan filled thine heart to lie to the Holy Ghost, and to keep back part of the price of the land? Whiles it remained, was it not thine own? and after it was sold, was it not in thine own power? why hast thou conceived this thing in thine heart? thou hast not lied unto men, but unto God. And Ananias hearing these words fell down, and gave up the ghost: and great fear came on all them that heard these things. And the young men arose, wound him up, and carried him out, and buried him. And it was about the space of three hours after, when his wife, not knowing what was done, came in. And Peter answered unto her, Tell me whether ye sold the land for so much? And she said, Yea, for so much. Then Peter said unto her, How is it that ye have agreed together to tempt the Spirit of the Lord? behold, the feet of them which have buried thy husband are at the door, and shall carry thee out. Then fell she down straightway at his feet, and yielded up the ghost: and the young men came in, and found her dead, and, carrying her forth, buried her by her husband. And great fear came upon all the church, and upon as many as heard these things.

Obviously, God takes lying to the Holy Spirit very seriously. Let's learn some important lessons from this passage:

Ananias and Sapphira conspired together to lie to God. The appearance was that they were giving the entire price of the land. In truth, they were only giving a portion. The amount of their offering was not the issue, for the land was "in their power." Their decision to live a lie was what offended God's Spirit. Their sin was not in keeping a portion of the sale. Their sin was in disobeying the Spirit and projecting a lie.

It is possible to masquerade a Spirit-filled life. This couple plotted hypocrisy. They decided to *appear* to be something, rather than to walk truthfully and genuinely with the Spirit. Amazingly, from the early days of Christianity, people have been trying to fake the Spirit-filled life—to put up a false front of spirituality. By the outcome of the story, we can see that God wants us to actually fear this sort of deception. He desires for us to be sincere, without offense, until the day of Christ (Philippians 1:10).

God is repulsed by a lack of spiritual authenticity. We see this not only in Acts 5, but also in Revelation 3:16 where the lukewarm condition of the Laodicean Christians actually caused God to want to "spue" them out of his mouth. A lack of authenticity in the Christian life makes God "sick to his stomach." In the case of Ananias and Sapphira, He allowed their deaths to be a public example so that fear came upon all the Christians. The message was loud and clear—when it comes to a spiritual life, *don't fake it!*

Lying to God's Spirit is a serious offense in the eyes of God. It's not about perfection, but rather sincerity. God knows you aren't perfect, but He expects you to be honest with Him and before others. Choose today that your heart and life will be truthful and authentic before God and man. Decide that you will develop a valid Christian life, and not merely an outward appearance of spirituality. The world doesn't need to see whitewashed exteriors of pious Christians pretending to be something they are not. The world needs to see God's Spirit in His power and fullness exhibited in your life through genuine fruit!

WE CAN QUENCH THE SPIRIT

The Bible gives this simple command in 1 Thessalonians 5:19, "Quench not the Spirit." The word *quench* means to extinguish or to put out. It's the idea of pouring water onto a fire. Have you ever sat by a fire for a long time? The flame changes over time. Without fuel it grows steadily dimmer. But as soon as you place more fuel into the flame, the fire begins to immediately grow and burn higher.

So is the work of the Holy Spirit in our lives—a fire. It is dynamic—constantly changing and desiring the fuel of a tender heart that it might continue burning more passionately. This fire is either growing hotter and burning brighter because you are fueling the fire of His presence, or it is growing colder and dimmer because you are quenching Him. Every moment of every day, you are either fueling the fire of His work or pouring water on it.

WE CAN GRIEVE THE SPIRIT

Ephesians 4:29–31 not only tells us that the Holy Spirit can be grieved, it lists specific sins that grieve Him, "Let no corrupt communication proceed out of your mouth, but that which is good to the use of edifying, that it may minister grace unto the hearers. And grieve not the holy Spirit of God, whereby ye are sealed unto the day of redemption. Let all bitterness, and wrath, and anger, and clamour, and evil speaking, be put away from you, with all malice."

The word *grieve* means to distress, to make sad, or to cause heaviness. This word provides such an intimate perspective on our daily relationship with the Lord. Do you marvel to think that you have the power to bring heaviness or sorrow to the Holy Spirit of God? This implies intimacy and closeness. It reminds us that God desires a close, personal fellowship with us. It is easiest to grieve those closest to you.

For instance, I thank the Lord for my wife Terrie and for the many years of marriage and love that God has given to us. In the busyness of life, I find that the single person I could most easily grieve is my dear wife—not because of a spirit of offense in her, but because our hearts are so closely knit in every area of life. When I discover that something I have done, or neglected to do, has grieved her, I want to make it right immediately. I don't want to live a single moment out of fellowship and closeness with Terrie. She's my best friend and closest companion.

The Holy Spirit is an even more intimate companion. And like a human relationship, He desires to live in close, sweet fellowship. God desires spiritual intimacy with your heart. The moment you sense you have done something to grieve the Holy Spirit, make it right. Be sensitive to His presence and desire to keep open communication with Him at all times.

D.L. Moody said, "I firmly believe that the moment our hearts are emptied of pride and selfishness and ambition and self-seeking and everything that is contrary to God's law, the Holy Ghost will come and fill every corner of our hearts; but if we are full of pride and conceit and ambition and self-seeking and pleasure and the world, there is no room for the Spirit of God; and I believe many a man is praying to God to fill him when he is full already with something else."

> The moment you sense you have done something to grieve the Holy Spirit, make it right.

When the Holy Spirit is grieved, the fire of His work starts to go out. He is restrained from working and His fruit will not grow. When this happens you will know it. You will sense the coldness and distance between your heart and the Holy Spirit. You will miss that intimate relationship. You may need to ask Him to search your heart and reveal to you what needs to be made right. Don't ignore this experience, for over time you could become calloused to it and even stop sensing His grief and conviction. Don't prolong the grief. Don't allow your conscience to become seared and insensitive. Confess the sin and restore fellowship with the Spirit of God as quickly as possible.

RESISTING AND BLASPHEMING THE SPIRIT

There are two final sins against the Holy Spirit that do not apply to Christians. In the context of Scripture, these are sins that unsaved men commit against the Spirit.

Resisting the Holy Spirit. In Acts 7:51 Stephen declared, "Ye stiffnecked and uncircumcised in heart and ears, ye do always resist the Holy Ghost: as your fathers did, so do ye." In this case, men were resisting the conviction and invitation of the Holy Spirit. They were opposed to what God was saying to them in their hearts. When an unsaved man comes under the convicting power of the Holy Spirit, he must make a choice—respond with an open heart and receive what the Holy Spirit is saying, or resist it and oppose it.

It's a dangerous thing for a lost man to resist the Holy Spirit. For that man never knows if the Spirit will speak to him again in the same way. He may be resisting his last opportunity to be saved.

Blaspheming the Holy Spirit. In Matthew 12:31 we read of the second sin, blasphemy against the Holy Ghost. "Wherefore I say unto you, All manner of sin and blasphemy shall be forgiven unto men: but the blasphemy against the Holy Ghost shall not be forgiven unto men."

To *blaspheme* means to vilify or to speak impiously. It is to fully reject with absolute scorn and disdain—to absolutely deny. This is very much what atheists, apostates, and pagans do in the face of God. Many men go beyond resisting the Spirit. They actually spit in God's face and reject Him outright, even with anger. This is the "unpardonable sin" that so many misunderstand today.

Simply put, God's offer of salvation is for "whosoever *will*." Revelation 22:17, "And the Spirit and the bride say, Come. And let him that heareth say, Come. And let him that is athirst come. And whosoever will, let him take the water of life freely."

God gives every man the *free will* to choose or reject Christ. Those who *will* to be saved, can be saved. Those who *will not* to be saved, cannot be saved. And blasphemy against the Holy Spirit is the deliberate choice of the will to say "no." It is the choice to defiantly *will not* to be saved. God saves no man *against* his will, but God saves every man who is *willing* to be saved!

If you haven't yet trusted Christ as Saviour, then once again, I implore you—please do not resist or reject the Holy Spirit's conviction in your heart. Accept His invitation to salvation right now.

If you have already trusted Christ, then heed God's warnings about these sins so that you don't prohibit His work in your life. C.H. Spurgeon eloquently said, "Without the Spirit of God we can do nothing. We are as ships without wind or chariots without steeds. Like branches without sap, we are withered. Like coals without fire, we are useless. As an offering without the sacrificial flame, we are unaccepted."

When we make a habit of offending the Holy Spirit, we are robbing ourselves of the greatest joys of the Christian life. Think of all of the marvelous ministries and works of the Spirit that we have studied. What Christian wouldn't desire to let that fire burn freely? Why would you choose to lie, quench, or grieve such a wonderful, transcendent companion?

TWELVE

THE SPIRIT-FILLED LIFE

Early in my pastoral ministry at Lancaster Baptist Church, the Lord allowed me to preach at a meeting in Northern California with Dr. Lee Roberson. He was the pastor of Highland Park Baptist Church for many years, and the founder of Tennessee Temple University in Chattanooga, Tennessee. As a young pastor, I was eager to spend some time with Dr. Roberson and to receive counsel from him regarding our growing, young church.

Finally, the moment came when I was alone with him. With a yellow pad in hand, and a heart full of questions, I was ready to vigorously take note of every word. I was certain I would leave the appointment with several pages of notes to implement in my life and local church.

I don't recall what my first question was, but I will never forget his answer. With his trademark tone of voice, and with firm but brief certainty, he simply said, "Die to self and be filled with the Holy Spirit." This wasn't quite the profound, lengthy, detailed answer I had anticipated. It struck me as overly simplistic and left me wanting a longer discussion about the problem. But I wasn't about to question this great man. I wrote the answer down and moved on to the next question.

Once again, and with the same tone of voice, his resolute answer was, "Die to self and be filled with the Holy Spirit." Can you believe this continued for several more questions? His pat answer to nearly every single question was the same, "Die to self and be filled with the Holy Spirit."

What at first seemed overly simplistic, became a transforming truth to my entire life and ministry. God knew exactly what I needed to hear, and He let me hear it over and over that day. I will never forget that meeting. It changed everything about my approach to the Christian life and ministry. It was without hesitation, the greatest advice I have ever been given.

When D.L. Moody was just starting in the ministry, he heard a preacher make this statement, "The world has yet to see what God can do with a man fully surrendered to Him." Moody that night said, "By God's grace, I'll be that man!" It is said that Moody shook two continents for God and over a million souls came to Christ under his preaching and ministry.

Will you have the heart that D.L. Moody had? Will you give the Holy Spirit absolute prominence in your life? He deserves full and absolute control. He is God in you. You belong to Him. You are His vessel and His ambassador. It is reasonable Christianity that you would surrender complete control of your daily life to His power.

Romans 12:1 teaches this, "I beseech you therefore, brethren, by the mercies of God, that ye present your bodies a living sacrifice, holy, acceptable unto God, which is your reasonable service."

Knowing about the Holy Spirit is quite different from experiencing Him at work in your life.

The Holy Spirit will bring transformation and power into your life that you could otherwise never know. He will lead you into a life abundant and full—a life beyond your capacity. Jesus said in John 10:10, "The thief cometh not, but for to steal, and to kill, and to destroy: I am come that they might have life, and that they might have it more abundantly." This abundant life, known by so few Christians, is the product of the Holy Spirit.

In these final two chapters, we will discover how to have this abundant life that Jesus promised. We will discover how to fully immerse ourselves in a daily, Spirit-filled, Spirit-led lifestyle. After studying this far, I pray you are eager to experience all that God desires to do in you by His Spirit. These simple principles are the "how to" of Spirit-filled living.

Living a Spirit-filled life is about learning how to *practice His presence* moment by moment. It's a daily discipline and a daily choice not to neglect Him. C.H. Spurgeon said, "The greatest crime of sinners is to blaspheme the Holy Ghost, and the greatest fault of saints is to neglect the Holy Ghost."

In a few minutes you will set this book down and your life will go on. At that moment, you will make a decision. Will you neglect Him or will you be filled with Him? Have these pages merely provided you with a good head knowledge of some very profound possibilities? Or will the daily practices of your life change because of what you have read? *Knowing about* the Holy Spirit is quite different from *experiencing* Him at work in your life. You could live beyond your capacity, but it's up to you to avail yourself of the Spirit. It's up to you to surrender yourself to Him and to choose to fellowship with Him continuously.

Many are ignorant of Him. Most neglect Him. What will you do? The Bible gives us three commands regarding our response to the Spirit:

BE FILLED WITH THE SPIRIT

This Bible command is found in Ephesians 5:18, "And be not drunk with wine, wherein is excess; but be filled with the Spirit." Being filled with the Spirit is the act of emptying myself of known sin, and yielding myself completely to the Holy Spirit. It is an act of the will. It is an act of surrender in prayer. It is not sensational and does not provide a feeling or exhilarating experience. It is a decision of faith to yield complete control of myself to the Spirit. We sometimes see this in Scripture as *dying to self*— "I am crucified with Christ: nevertheless I live; yet not I, but Christ liveth in me: and the life which I now live in the flesh I live by the faith of the Son of God, who loved me, and gave himself for me" (Galatians 2:20).

Romans 6:12–13 teaches us, "Let not sin therefore reign in your mortal body, that ye should obey it in the lusts thereof. Neither yield ye your members as instruments of unrighteousness unto sin: but yield yourselves unto God, as those that are alive from the dead, and your members as instruments of righteousness unto God."

And Romans 6:16 says, "Know ye not, that to whom ye yield yourselves servants to obey, his servants ye are to whom ye obey; whether of sin unto death, or of obedience unto righteousness?"

These passages teach us that we must constantly choose who to "yield to." We live every day either in the service of the flesh or the control of the Spirit. Most Christians do not willfully choose to walk in the flesh, but they arrive there by *default* because they fail to deliberately yield to the Spirit.

Speaking to a large audience, D.L. Moody held up a glass and asked, "How can I get the air out of this glass?" One man shouted, "Suck it out with a pump!" Moody replied, "That would create a vacuum and shatter the glass." After numerous other suggestions

Moody smiled, picked up a pitcher of water, and filled the glass. "There," he said, "all the air is now removed."

Even so, as we empty ourselves of known sin and yield to the Holy Spirit, He will fill us completely. The victorious Christian life is attained when the Holy Spirit has the whole pitcher in which to dwell and not just a part of it. How do we go about giving the Holy Spirit the whole pitcher? It's a daily decision. Here are a few practical steps to being filled with the Spirit:

Being filled with the Spirit is a daily decision. Begin every day by consciously and verbally yielding to the Holy Spirit of God. Ask Him to fill you and control you throughout the day. Acknowledge His presence and Lordship in your life. Acknowledge that you need Him.

Consider beginning every day by praying something like this: *"Holy Spirit of God, thank You for being my comforter and guide today. As best as I know how, I yield myself to You right now. I ask You to fill me, control me, lead me, and guide me. I need You today. I choose to be the servant of righteousness. I choose to follow Your call. I choose to live in the Spirit, to be spiritually minded, and I ask You to have complete control of my life as I serve You today."*

Being filled with the Spirit is moment-by-moment. As we've already studied, the Holy Spirit of God can be quenched and grieved. Therefore being Spirit-filled requires moment-by-moment sensitivity. The moment I step out of His control, I should confess it and ask Him to fill me once again.

Being filled with the Spirit is "by faith." The filling of the Spirit is not a feeling, it is a faith decision. You ask for it, you yield, and then you accept by faith that it is done. The moment you yield to the Spirit and ask Him to fill you, accept by faith that He has answered your prayer, regardless of how you feel. Guaranteed, a day lived in the filling of the Holy Spirit is dramatically different from one lived without Him. You may not feel all that different throughout your day, but you will know by the day's end that the Holy Spirit guided your steps, filtered your thinking, directed your words, and ordered your life.

Being filled with the Spirit helps me grow in developing the mind of Christ. Philippians 2:5, "Let this mind be in you, which was also in Christ Jesus." With every passing day that you consciously yield to the filling of the Holy Spirit, you are growing and maturing in Christ. You are being transformed into His image. Day by day, you may not feel like you are growing, but year by year, you will be able to look back and see great transformation.

Remember how you used to measure growth as a kid by marking your height on a doorway or wall? Day to day those markings wouldn't change much. But year after year, the growth became evident. Have patience as you yield to the Holy Spirit. His work is intended to take a lifetime. The Christian life is a marathon, not a sprint.

Being filled with the Spirit is about repentance, restoration, and forgiveness. When you sin against God and break your close fellowship with Him, He invites you to make things right. He invites you to come back into fellowship—to restore your heart to Him. Psalm 51:10 says, "Create in me a clean heart, O God; and renew a right spirit within me."

Living a Spirit-filled life requires a quick response to sin. Acknowledge to God when you have offended Him. Accept His forgiveness. Be restored by confessing sin and then re-enter the Spirit-filled life by faith and continue growing in God's grace. The Spirit-filled life runs from sin and embraces holiness.

> Have patience as you yield to the Holy Spirit. His work is intended to take a lifetime.

Being filled with the Holy Spirit is not getting more and more of the Spirit, but the Spirit getting more and more of me. F.B. Meyer said it this way, "Do not pray for more of the Holy Spirit. The Holy Spirit is the Third Person of the Trinity and is not in pieces. Every child of God has all of Him, but does He have all of us?"

The filling of the Spirit is the constant pursuit of the Christian life—living in a perpetual state of total surrender and submission. It is a daily discipline that chooses to include the Holy Spirit rather than neglect Him.

I love this prayer from Betty Scott Stam, "Lord, I give up all my own plans and purposes, all my own desires and hopes, and accept Thy will for my life. I give myself, my life, my all utterly to Thee to be Thine forever. Fill me and seal me with Thy Holy Spirit. Use me as Thou wilt. Send me where Thou wilt. Work out Thy whole will in my life at any cost, now and forever."

WALK IN THE SPIRIT

Earlier we talked about the daily decision to be filled with the Spirit. This filling will produce a daily walk—a lifestyle that is led by the Spirit. We see this command in Galatians 5:16, "This I say then, Walk in the Spirit, and ye shall not fulfil the lust of the flesh." And again in Galatians 5:25, "If we live in the Spirit, let us also walk in the Spirit." Also, Romans 8:1 states, "There is therefore now no condemnation to them which are in Christ Jesus, who walk not after the flesh, but after the Spirit."

Walking in the Spirit is the natural result of being filled with the Spirit. The word *walk* implies to march in step with, to fall into rank, or to conform to the virtue of. In the Bible, the word *walk* is often used to reference your daily lifestyle. This boils down to your everyday choices.

Think of it this way: When you begin your day by asking the Holy Spirit to fill you, He will. Your choice to yield control is a good choice. It's the right start. But as your day unfolds you will face a myriad of circumstances, emotions, thoughts, feelings, desires, decisions, and possibilities. Walking in the Spirit is the developed discipline of listening to and obeying Him in the minutia of your daily life.

The Spirit is interested in what you think about, what you listen to, what you watch, what you read, what you say, how you act, and who you spend time with. In every possible situation, you must choose between the will of the flesh and the will of the Spirit. Walking in the Spirit is to listen to His prompting and obey it. On the other hand, walking in the flesh is to give in to your carnal impulses and desires.

Most Christians ignore and neglect the Spirit and walk in the flesh. That is not to say that they do not love God, trust His Word, or believe in His power. It's to say they don't cultivate the discipline to listen to the Holy Spirit and obey Him moment by moment.

God delights in the fact that you remember Him—that you include Him, call upon Him, and obey Him. Hear His heart in Jeremiah 2:32 as He longs to be a part of your every moment— "Can a maid forget her ornaments, or a bride her attire? yet my people have forgotten me days without number." How many days have passed since you remembered to walk in the Spirit? Why not begin walking with Him today?

In every choice you make, you either choose to hear and obey the Spirit, or you choose a carnal life. You could downplay the little decisions of life and think, "It's really not that big of a deal." But little decisions, when put together, make a life. A messed up life is just a whole bunch of bad decisions put together. A blessed life is a whole bunch of good decisions put together. The Holy Spirit wants to lead and direct you into every good decision, but the choice to walk in the Spirit is yours.

My kids are all grown, but how I would love to go back and take a few more family strolls. It would be great to rewind the clock and recapture time together. With every passing day, you have one less day to walk with God. Don't live your life having neglected this great privilege.

I challenge you to develop a lifestyle of walking in the Spirit. There will be resistance from the flesh, but the Holy Spirit will be there to help and guide you. The Spirit-filled, Spirit-led life is the very best possible life you could ever experience. D.L. Moody once said, "A Christian who is not living in the power of the Spirit is living below his privileges."

Reader's Digest published an interesting story in March of 2005 about Hyper Sonic Sound (or HSS). The inventor, Elwood "Woody" Norris, has engineered sound waves to travel like a laser beam for about 150 yards. This allows sounds to be heard by a person in a particular place but not by those immediately around them.

God's communication with us is very similar to these sound waves. We must be walking with the Holy Spirit in order to hear Him. And when we're walking with the Spirit, His communications are clear. It's easy to perceive what He is saying. If we move away from the pathway of His voice, we become unaware of the fact that

He is communicating with us at all, and we consequently miss the message.

If you will begin your day tomorrow by yielding to the Holy Spirit and asking Him to fill you, and if you will intend to hear His prompting and obey, I promise you will hear Him well throughout the day. He's a very good communicator.

Walk in the Spirit today and every day. Be intentional about it. First Corinthians 2:15 begins with these convicting words, "But he that is spiritual…." Let that be you.

PRAY IN THE SPIRIT

Do you ever take walks? How about walks with a friend? I love to walk with Terrie—unless it's at a shopping mall. I'm not much of a shopper. But put us in a beautiful park or a pristine stretch of Southern California coastline at dusk, and I could walk for eternity with my wonderful wife. I've noticed something about walks. They naturally lead to conversation. As I walk with Terrie, we talk, we grow closer, and we experience a stronger relationship together.

This third command to pray in the Spirit should be the natural outflow of walking with the Spirit. If I'm filled with the Spirit and walking with Him, then it's quite natural to converse. And the more I walk with Him, the more normal it becomes to talk with Him throughout the day. Hence God's command to "pray without ceasing" (1 Thessalonians 5:17).

One of the greatest spiritual exercises you can do with the help of the Holy Spirit is pray. It's more than a conversation. It's a building, growing, battling endeavor. It's a vital part of winning the spiritual warfare of the Christian life.

Jude 20 says, "But ye, beloved, building up yourselves on your most holy faith, praying in the Holy Ghost." The book of Jude was written to Christians under fire. It's written to challenge Christians to earnestly contend for the faith of Christ and to fight the daily spiritual battle of faithfulness. Toward the end of the book, we read this command to build up ourselves in the faith by praying in the Holy Ghost.

Also the Apostle Paul, writing of spiritual battle, pleaded with believers in Ephesians 6:18–19, "Praying always with all prayer and supplication in the Spirit, and watching thereunto with all perseverance and supplication for all saints; And for me, that utterance may be given unto me, that I may open my mouth boldly, to make known the mystery of the gospel." Just after a lengthy passage about spiritual warfare, the Bible commands us to pray "always with all prayer and supplication in the Spirit...." This ongoing conversation with the Holy Spirit plays a significant role in winning the moment-by-moment struggle between the flesh and the Spirit.

E.M. Bounds was a man who understood the power of prayer. He wrote, "What the church needs today is not more machinery or better, not new organizations or more and novel methods, but men whom the Holy Spirit can use—men of prayer, mighty in prayer. The Holy Spirit does not flow through methods, but through men. He does not come on machinery, but on men. He does not anoint plans, but men—men of prayer."

We've already seen that the Holy Spirit is our partner in prayer—our intercessor. This command compels us once more to enter into ongoing and intimate communion with the Father by the Holy Spirit. It is more than a command. It is a compelling invitation that triggers the Spirit's ongoing work.

Because of what Christ did on the Cross, God invites us into moment-by-moment prayer and personal intercession with Him— Hebrews 4:16, "Let us therefore [because of what Christ did] come boldly unto the throne of grace, that we may obtain mercy, and find grace to help in time of need."

What an awesome thought! By the Spirit, God invites me to have an ongoing conversation and free flowing intercession with Him all day, every day. The more you practice His presence in this way and come boldly before Him, the more victorious you will be in the daily struggle.

If you're thinking, "I would love to experience this ongoing life of walking in the Spirit and praying in the Spirit, but I forget"—don't despair. Remember, the Christian life is a journey of growth and learning. This life of prayer is a learned discipline. It's a developed habit. Start right now. Ask the Holy Spirit to remind you. Ask Him to teach you. Cry out to God and claim His help in developing these spiritual habits. Over time, you will. The day will eventually come when you will probably talk more to the Holy Spirit than you do to any other person in your life. He's with you every moment and you will remember and acknowledge Him constantly.

In summary, the Spirit-filled life is a life of three basic but powerful daily disciplines:

Being filled with the Spirit is the deliberate choice to yield all of myself to His control.

Walking in the Spirit is the moment-by-moment choice to hear and obey His prompting.

Praying in the Spirit is entering into spiritual warfare in partnership with the Holy Spirit through ongoing prayer. It's the act of faithfully coming before my Heavenly Father to commune with Him personally and to seek His power and protection.

This life of prayer is a learned discipline.

This is the Christian life in a nutshell—yield to the Spirit, walk in the Spirit, and pray in the Spirit. Give God control every day, obey Him in the moments, and learn to speak to Him continually. This is the Spirit-filled life, and it is the only path to all of the fullness of the Spirit that we have studied in this book.

One of my favorite ways to illustrate the Holy Spirit and the Christian came from a godly lady named Corrie ten Boom. The illustration requires only a simple leather gardening glove. By itself, the glove is just a piece of cloth. It is limp and lifeless—powerless. But when I pick up that glove and place my hand into it, the glove comes to life. It can accomplish much when filled with a hand. It can fulfill the purposes of the one who is wearing it.

Like the empty glove, I am nothing but flesh—spiritually dead and useless. But one day God saved my soul and sent His Spirit into my life. He picked up my life and placed His hand in it. And because of God's hand within me, I can now accomplish all that He created me to accomplish.

If I accomplish anything in my life, it is not me, for I am just a glove. It is the power of God, the hand of God within me.

You are the glove, and the Holy Spirit is the hand. Make room for the Holy Spirit. Choose to yield to Him, walk in Him, and pray in Him, that every finger of your life might be filled with His awesome presence every day!

THIRTEEN

A PORTRAIT OF A SPIRIT-FILLED MAN

Heavyweight boxing champion Muhammad Ali was not known for his humility. Having won three separate heavyweight titles during his career, Ali often declared, "I'm the greatest!"

The story is told that one day Ali was sitting on an airplane preparing to take off. In preparation for the flight, the attendant stopped at Ali's seat, noticed that he was not buckled, and said, "Please buckle your seat belt."

Ali, in his typically over-confident manner, quipped, "Superman don't need no seat belt."

To which the flight attendant retorted, "Superman don't need no airplane either. Now buckle your seat belt."

When it comes to living the Christian life, nobody is Superman. We are all utterly dependent upon God's power to accomplish God's will. Being Spirit-filled has nothing to do with your own greatness or your own ability. It is all about Him! It is complete humility coupled with utter dependency.

What does a Spirit-filled life look like in everyday life? Is there a way that we can open God's Word, and examine a Spirit-filled life up close? I believe there is. The Bible has much to say about men who were filled with the Holy Spirit, and God gives us very practical insight into the behavior, the thinking, and the responses of a Spirit-filled man.

One of the greatest examples of Spirit-filled living is the man Stephen. Acts 6:1–8 gives us a glimpse of this man. He was not an apostle. He was not in full-time, vocational ministry. But he was a faithful man who was filled with the Holy Spirit. Carefully consider his story:

> *And in those days, when the number of the disciples was multiplied, there arose a murmuring of the Grecians against the Hebrews, because their widows were neglected in the daily ministration. Then the twelve called the multitude of the disciples unto them, and said, It is not reason that we should leave the word of God, and serve tables. Wherefore, brethren, look ye out among you seven men of honest report, full of the Holy Ghost and wisdom, whom we may appoint over this business. But we will give ourselves*

continually to prayer, and to the ministry of the word.
And the saying pleased the whole multitude: and
they chose Stephen, a man full of faith and of the
Holy Ghost, and Philip, and Prochorus, and Nicanor,
and Timon, and Parmenas, and Nicolas a proselyte
of Antioch: Whom they set before the apostles: and
when they had prayed, they laid their hands on them.
And the word of God increased; and the number of
the disciples multiplied in Jerusalem greatly; and a
great company of the priests were obedient to the
faith. And Stephen, full of faith and power, did great
wonders and miracles among the people.

Remember, Stephen was a member of a local church. His story applies to every Christian. Let's take a closer look and see what the Spirit's filling looked like in his life:

THE MINISTRY OF A SPIRIT-FILLED MAN

The early churches of the book of Acts were growing. The number of disciples was rapidly multiplying. This is a good problem, but there were some negative aspects of growth. The leaders were stretched too thin and the needs of the people were multiplying. As a result, the widows of the church were not being cared for properly and it was causing a lot of frustration—the people were murmuring and grumbling about it.

The apostles called an assembly and explained that their primary calling was to the teaching and preaching of the Word of God. Their solution was to select seven men—honest, wise, Spirit-filled men—who could be appointed to care for these needs within the church family. The plan worked! The men were selected and commissioned, the people were pleased, and the apostles were able to focus on the ministry of the Word. The result in verse 7 was that the Word of God increased and the number of the disciples multiplied greatly. Even a great number of Jewish priests were coming to faith in Christ.

Stephen was among the men chosen to serve. Notice what God says about him:

Stephen was a leader in his local church. We know this because he was chosen, and he was identified as honest, wise, and Spirit-filled. When the early church looked around the church body, Stephen was among the "good guys." He was one that stood out as genuinely spiritual. He was authentic. He obviously had a good report among the church family. Everybody who knew Stephen knew he was a good man.

Stephen was full of faith. Stephen had a full persuasion of the Lord. His life publicly declared that he trusted God and believed in God's power. The Holy Spirit was developing the fruit of faithfulness, and it made Stephen a servant and a leader in his church.

Stephen was full of the Holy Ghost. The filling of the Spirit in Stephen's life was evident to others. His public life was the manifestation of a private walk with God.

Stephen was full of power. In Stephen's case, the Holy Spirit enabled him with sign gifts. He performed miracles and wonders among the people. As we stated, these same sign gifts are not continuing today, but God's power certainly is. And when His power is outpoured through your life, the results will be obviously beyond human capacity.

> When you serve God in the power and fullness of His Spirit, the results will be bigger than you.

The results of Stephen's life and ministry were evidently anointed—beyond his own capacity. When people studied Stephen's ministry, they would have asked, "Wow, how did you do that?" And his answer would have been, "I didn't. It's the Spirit of God within me."

Even so, when you serve God in the power and fullness of His Spirit, the results will be bigger than you. When God does something special, people will step back and wonder how it's being done. They will perhaps attempt to give you credit. They will ask, "How are you doing that?" And your only reasonable answer will be, "Not by might, nor by power, but by [His] spirit" (Zechariah 4:6)! All the results are of God and for God's glory. Acts 1:8, "But ye shall receive power, after that the Holy Ghost is come upon you...."

THE MESSAGE OF THE SPIRIT-FILLED MAN

Not only was Stephen's ministry incredibly effective, but his message was unique. He was a man on a mission, and as soon as he was placed into leadership, God began to use him to speak the truth. The rest of chapter 6 unfolds a remarkable story of what God did with this man.

Because the Word of God was increasing, and many were coming to Christ, especially many priests, the various religious groups and their leaders were becoming increasingly threatened and angry with Stephen. This man was making a difference, and people were noticing—especially the opposition. Stephen became a target. He was a man that the opposition wanted to silence.

Over a period of time, Stephen was disputing with these leaders in the synagogue and preaching of Christ. These religious leaders were in the habit of debating religion with unregenerate men. This was perhaps their first experience in debating with a Spirit-filled man, and they didn't like the result. The Bible says in verse 10, "And they were not able to resist the wisdom and the spirit by which he spake." These men were put to open shame before the common, unlearned man Stephen—church-member-turned-teacher by God's Holy Spirit. He had not been through the schools of religion. He was not a "professional religious leader." He was a man filled with the Spirit.

The religious leaders became so desperate to silence Stephen that they finally resorted to hiring liars to come in and accuse him of blasphemy—in that day, a crime punishable by death. The conspiracy continued as the hired men stirred up a crowd of followers, went and took Stephen into custody, and forced him into a mock council that was framed against him. They proceeded to parade false accusers and lying witnesses before the council. It was an angry, tragic, and unbelievable miscarriage of justice and defamation—all against a man with a spotless name and flawless personal walk.

Amidst the madness and mayhem of this bogus trial, the Spirit-filled man had quite a different response than we would expect. We read in verse 15, "And all that sat in the council, looking steadfastly on him, saw his face as it had been the face of an angel."

Angelic! No further comment needed.

It's not until chapter 7 that Stephen begins to answer for himself. Finally, we hear his message. When we should expect self-defense, self-justification, and rebuttal to his false accusers, we find the message of a Spirit-filled man to be quite the opposite.

Stephen's message was filled with the Word of God. He spoke the truth of God with boldness. He stood and preached to them of Israel's perpetual history of idolatry and resistance of the Holy Spirit. His message was not of self defense or self preservation.

Theodore Roosevelt wisely said, "Almost every man who by his life-work added to the sum of human achievement of which the race is proud, of which our people are proud, almost every such man has based his life-work largely upon the teachings of the Bible." A Spirit-filled man has a Bible-centered message.

Stephen's message was fervent in opposition. In the midst of an angry mob and slanderous accusations, Stephen's spirit was unmoved and fervent for His Saviour. He was not swayed or dismayed by public opinion. So, when God's Spirit fills a man, he has new courage and strength to withstand and press on through the opposition.

Someone wisely said, "The men and women who have moved the world have been the men and women the world could not move."

Stephen's message was focused on Christ. He defended the testimony of Christ as he shared the story of Israel's history. His purpose was to show that the children of Israel did not always have a temple. Even as he was being stoned, he exalted Christ and pointed men to salvation.

Because of the filling of God's Spirit, Stephen made a difference—through his ministry, through his message, and through his manner.

THE MANNER OF A SPIRIT-FILLED MAN

Stephen was a man of purpose. He was not easily swayed by whim or emotion. He had a focused clarity about who he was in Christ and what God had called him to do. The Spirit gave him an intentional purpose in life. The Spirit gave him a ministry, a message, and a manner quite unusual for a man in his circumstances. You might say Stephen was certainly living beyond his capacity.

When most men would have been angry, vindictive, or vengeful, the Spirit-filled man was altogether different.

Stephen was bold in preaching. He knew the risk he was taking to say the things he said. He knew the probable outcome. But in spite of this, God's Spirit gave Stephen boldness to say what needed to be said. He was willing to be confrontational because that's what the situation required.

Boldness is a common denominator in men who are filled with the Holy Spirit: "And when they had prayed, the place was shaken where they were assembled together; and they were all filled with the Holy Ghost, and they spake the word of God with boldness" (Acts 4:31).

Stephen was gracious under pressure. The Sanhedrin, before whom he preached, did not see hate or horror in this man. They saw Heaven. His spirit was not angry, it was angelic. When the Holy Spirit fills a man, his manner is gracious. Acts 4:33 also indicates this, "And with great power gave the apostles witness of the resurrection of the Lord Jesus: and great grace was upon them all." "Great grace" is upon someone who is yielding to the power of the Spirit.

When you are mistreated, what do you do? Do you fire back? Do you plot for revenge? Or do you display "great grace"?

Stephen was a faithful witness. He witnessed for Christ, even while he was dying. He prayed for his murderers as they were stoning him. The Holy Spirit will make you a soulwinner, even in the most difficult of circumstances.

I have been at the bedsides of many Christian friends during their last moments of life. The final breaths of a Spirit-filled Christian are always focused on helping others to know Christ. It's amazing! In every case I have witnessed, a Spirit-filled Christian close to death always tried to witness and share Scripture with a nurse or doctor. I've watched them give a Gospel tract, a church invitation, and even ask others to share the Gospel with them. How is it possible that a dying Christian could have such care and concern for others? Only by His Spirit.

> The Holy Spirit will make you a soulwinner, even in the most difficult of circumstances.

Stephen was a forgiving martyr. He forgave those who killed him, and asked God to forgive them as well. In his final breaths, with stones crushing life from his body, he uttered forgiving words, and in doing so left an indelible mark on the soul of Saul who would soon be saved. Saul would become the great Apostle Paul and take the Gospel to the known world. It all began through the ministry, message, and manner of this Spirit-filled man, Stephen.

One of the most glaring indicators that the Holy Spirit isn't in control of a believer's life is an unforgiving spirit. When the Holy Spirit is at work, a gracious heart of forgiveness is evident at times when vengeance and spite would be a more natural and immediate response.

As we dissect Stephen's story, we see a life of servant leadership in his church. We see a life message focused on the Word of God and Jesus Christ. And we see a manner of uncommon grace and forgiveness.

How does your life measure up to this man's example? You probably haven't been called to die for Christ as Stephen was. But are you living for Him as Stephen did? Is the Spirit of God filling you and producing through you a ministry, a message, and a manner that is beyond your capacity?

Left to ourselves, our ministry ceases, for we have no desire to serve anyone but self. Our message also centers on self-promotion and our selfish agenda. And our manner becomes carnal, defensive, and harsh—the antithesis of "great grace."

Consider Stephen, and ask God to fill you with this same Holy Spirit. Ask God to lift you to a life beyond your capacity. Anybody can be dominated by the flesh. Rare is the Christian who exemplifies true Spirit-filling as Stephen did. When scorned, they serve. When falsely accused, they speak God's Word with boldness. When abused and tortured, they forgive with "great grace."

Is this possible in your life? It is—but only by the Spirit of God. "Ye are of God, little children, and have overcome them: because greater is he that is in you, than he that is in the world" (1 John 4:4).

CONCLUSION

LIVING BEYOND
YOUR CAPACITY

The Old Testament prophet, Zechariah, was called to serve God during the second year of Darius, King of Persia. This was during a time of tremendous national discouragement and despair for the nation of Israel. Prior to the writing of the book of Zechariah, the Jews had begun to return to Jerusalem from captivity and were attempting to rebuild the temple. Opposition was fierce and the work had ceased. For sixteen years, the temple was nothing more than a foundation. The nation was disgraced, the people were disheartened, and the odds of restoring the temple were slim.

For four years, God used the preaching of Haggai and Zechariah to stir the people to action and obedience. God's purpose was for the temple to be restored, and He used three key leaders to accomplish this purpose.

The first was Zechariah the prophet. He was a young man whose name means, "Jehovah remembers." God called Zechariah to help the people remember His power and promises. He called Zechariah to preach to the people that they might be stirred out of apathy and finish the rebuilding. His was a ministry of encouragement—revealing God's power and provision to the nation of Israel and encouraging them to trust Him.

The second was Zerubbabel the governor. This man was the head of the tribe of Judah at the time that they returned from Babylon to Jerusalem. He was a man that God raised up to lead the rebuilding. When he arrived at Jerusalem, he began this work immediately, but for sixteen years the work was stalled under Zerubbabel's leadership. God intended to stir Zerubbabel back to action through the preaching of Zechariah.

The third was Joshua the high priest (not the Joshua of the early Old Testament). Joshua was a key spiritual leader to the Jews who were returning to Jerusalem from captivity. He worked alongside Zerubbabel.

All three of these men hold a pivotal place in the history of the nation of Israel. Their lives converged at a critical time, and God used each one in a very unique way. Zerubbabel and Joshua were facing insurmountable problems, and lacked resources for the rebuilding. The people were discouraged. The nation was in disarray. And the work of God was halted. With these problems, the completing of the temple would have seemed as impossible as moving a mountain. But God had other plans. He intended to empower these men and the people so that the mountain would indeed become a plain: "Who art thou, O great mountain? before Zerubbabel thou shalt become a plain: and he shall bring forth the headstone thereof with shoutings, crying, Grace, grace unto it" (Zechariah 4:7). God's power was about to be manifested through these men. The mountain would indeed be moved by God's Spirit.

In Zechariah 4:2–3 we read of a vision that God gave to Zechariah concerning the work of rebuilding the temple. The vision was one of two golden lamp stands:

> And said unto me, What seest thou? And I said, I have looked, and behold a candlestick all of gold, with a bowl upon the top of it, and his seven lamps thereon, and seven pipes to the seven lamps, which are upon the top thereof: And two olive trees by it, one upon the right side of the bowl, and the other upon the left side thereof.

In this vision, the lamp stand represents the nation of Israel. The oil represents the Holy Spirit. The vision shows two olive trees continually supplying olive oil into a bowl that indefinitely sustains the burning lamp stand. Unlike the lamp in the temple, which required the priest to provide the oil, this lamp stand had a continual flow of oil from the olive trees.

The light of the lamp stand (metaphorically speaking) was burning very low when the remnant of the Jews returned to Jerusalem. No one believed there was hope for the rebuilding and the restoration of God's people. But the astounding problems Zerubbabel and Joshua faced were not larger than the astounding power of God. The trees in the vision represented Zerubbabel and Joshua. And the oil from the trees, again, represented the Holy Spirit and the power of God.

> God's work can still be accomplished by His Spirit.

The vision becomes more clear in verse 6, "Then he answered and spake unto me, saying, This is the word of the LORD unto Zerubbabel, saying, Not by might, nor by power, but by my spirit, saith the LORD of hosts."

The word *might* refers to military might, what people can do together, but the remnant had no army. *Power* refers to the strength of the individual, but Zerubbabel's strength was no doubt waning. "Don't be discouraged!" was the prophet's message. "The Spirit of God will enable us to do what an army could never do!" Had they forgotten what Haggai said to them? Haggai 2:5, "According to the word that I covenanted with you when ye came out of Egypt, so my spirit remaineth among you: fear ye not."

The vision climaxes in Zechariah 4:14 with God calling Zerubbabel and Joshua, "Then said he, These are the two anointed ones, that stand by the Lord of the whole earth." What a noble title for His servants. As the two olive trees, Joshua and Zerubbabel received the empowering Spirit of God and kept the light of Israel's work and witness burning brightly.

Do you hear the heart of God in this powerful passage? "Not by might, nor by power, but by my spirit, saith the LORD of hosts." God's work in you, God's work in your church, and God's work in this dark day can still be accomplished by His Spirit.

The rest of the story is that God did what He promised. He poured out His unlimited power and supply upon these two men. He worked through their leadership to revive His people, restore their hearts for God, and rebuild the temple. In spite of the overwhelming odds, God's Spirit made it all happen.

God's people have always faced daunting circumstances. They have always been called to trust Him through trying times. For in the midst of those times, we discover that His Holy Spirit is what we truly need more than anything else.

As we come to the conclusion of this book, my heart is heavy for God's work and God's people all over the world. This world is not becoming more friendly toward Bible-believing Christians. Many are discouraged. Many are compromising the truth. Many are losing hope.

Like the Jews returning from captivity, the odds of accomplishing something great for God seem slim. Sometimes we are tempted to wonder if God still works in power. But resounding from the vision of Zechariah—from the voice of a young prophet of God—we read these words, "…Not by might, nor by power, but by my spirit, saith the LORD of hosts."

God's Holy Spirit is our limitless supply of power, strength, hope, and joy. He is our abundance during times of discouragement. He is our power as we attempt to do the will of God. He is our intercessor, our encourager, our comforter, and our faithful friend. He is our transcendent companion.

By His Spirit you can live with power and blessing. You can accomplish God's eternal purposes in your life. Zechariah did. Zerubbabel did. Joshua did. The same Spirit lives within you and calls you to a greater life right now.

You are not called to mediocrity. You are not called to discouragement or despair. You are not called to weariness or frustration. You are not called to carnality, sin, self-centered living, or cynicism. You are called to live beyond your capacity. You are called to a higher standard, a greater abundance, a supernatural power, and an extravagant joy. You are called to the Spirit-filled life!

You can look around and become discouraged. You can look within and see your own limitations. Or you can look up and see God's offer of fresh anointing from His Holy Spirit. Look up! Claim it! Walk with Him starting right now!

The Holy Spirit desires to walk with you through life—every moment of every day. Enter into that intimate walk. Yield to Him. Listen to Him. Rely upon Him. Hope in Him.

Begin today to live *beyond your capacity*, "...Not by might, nor by power, but by my spirit, saith the LORD of hosts" (Zechariah 4:6).

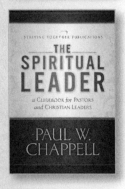
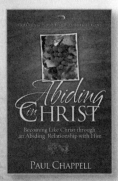

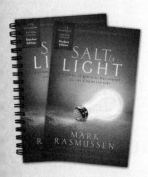

Visit us online

strivingtogether.com

wcbc.edu